A
JOURNEY
IN
SALVATION

A Theological Novel

Richard P. Belcher

Cover Photography by Ravenel Scott

ISBN 1-883265-22-3

Richbarry Press

P.O. Box 302   Columbia, SC 29202
         Phone: 803-750-0408   Fax: 803-798-3190
              E-Mail: docbelcher@juno.com
       Visit our web site at: www.richbarrypress.com

Printed in the Unites States of America

Contents

INDEX OF DOCTRINES

INDEX OF SCRIPTURE
(All verses and passages which are expounded or referenced)

1

Where Did That Question Originate?

I wasn't prepared for the question that my son, Ira, Jr. asked me that fall night in 1983.[1] One can anticipate many questions a child will ask, but there was no way I could ever have expected this one. But, first, some background to lay the foundation for the question.

We had moved to Seminary City in the summer of 1983, where I had been invited to join the faculty of the theology department of Evangelistic Baptist Theological Seminary, while I finished my doctoral studies. Of course, that meant resigning Unity Baptist Church in Collegetown, where I had served as pastor for over eleven years, while finishing various other degrees.

That was a heart-wrenching experience, leaving my beloved people at Unity, all except Dink, that is. He decided to resign his position in the church and come to Seminary City to work full-time on a doctorate in evangelism. Thus with my teaching and his presence as a student, we were together almost every day---as always.

But it also meant that Ira, Jr. at ten years of age changed schools, as he entered the fifth grade that fall. By now he had a little sister, Beth, who had been born in the Spring of 1982. Thus we were a happy settled family, I thought, on that October evening, when I finished up some work, and then went to say good night to Ira. Something seemed unusual that evening. He was not as talkative and as open as usual. But when I asked him if every thing was well, he replied in the affirmative, but I noticed, it was not with the greatest confidence. I prayed with him, and kissed him good night, and went back to grading some papers.

It was about an hour later, when I was going down the hall to get something from our bedroom, that I passed his door, and it sounded like he was crying. I stopped and listened for a few moments, and sure enough, he was crying his heart out, with overwhelming sobs.

I entered the room and immediately began to hug him and give him assurance, but also to ask him what was wrong. For several minutes he couldn't speak, though he tried, because of the uncontrollable and engulfing sobs. I continued to comfort him and urged him not to try to speak till he had settled down. Finally the weeping stopped, and I just held him for a few moments, sort of rocking him gently in my arms.

My mind began to search for some reason for this upheaval of emotions. Was it something I had said? Was it something his mother had said? Was it the presence of a younger child in the home? Was it something that had taken place at school? I couldn't recall any problem in his transition from one school to another. He seemed happy and well adjusted to his new environment, and even spoke of having made some new friends.

Was it his new teacher? She had seemed kind and even conservative in her thinking. Had the school brought in something of a liberal bias in practice or thought to infringe on his sensitive heart? He was a very delicate young soul, with a clear conviction of sin and a sense of morality based on the Scripture, having already professed faith in Christ.

Try as I did, I could not think of a single thing that could have triggered this! Thus not only were my emotions being stretched in this hour, when I felt so powerless to help him, but my thought process to find a solution was being short-circuited at every path my mind tried to take to trace the problem to its source.

Finally, he calmed down and just settled into my arms for a few minutes, not even trying to speak. He just looked drained and spent as he stared sadly into my face with a forlorn look that shook me to the depth of my being.

And then he spoke the question I could never have anticipated in all my days.

"Daddy, will you ever leave mommy and me and Beth to go be with another woman?!"

My only thought was, "Where in the world did that idea or question originate?"

I knew I had to deal with both the question and its origin and its damage!!

Daddy, Will You Help Me?

While I was waiting for Ira, Jr. to calm down, and to be able to speak coherently and without trembling, I assured him that by the grace of our great God such a thing would not happen. I further stated my love for him, and for mommy and for Beth. That seemed to settle him, and opened the door for my question.

"Son, what caused you to think that I or any one would do something like that?"

His answer was understandable.

He had made many new friends at his new school, but his best friend was a little girl named April, who was new also. They were in the same class, and ate lunch together every day. Today she didn't show up at lunch, even though she had been in class. After eating quickly, he went to look for her. He found her sitting under a tree crying.

When he asked her what the problem was, she began to cry even as I had found him crying.

"Daddy, I couldn't stop her from crying! And I couldn't get her to tell me why she was crying!"

Finally she spoke through her grief and tears and said, "Ira, my daddy needs someone to help him, but I don't know who to ask who might be able to help him."

Then she told young Ira that her daddy had left her mommy to be with another woman, and that he wasn't living with them any more. When he did come to their house, his visits always ended in a big fight with a lot of yelling at each other.

"Ira, I always go to my room and shut the door and cover my ears and cry!" she declared.

When young Ira asked her how long this had been going on, she replied for several weeks, but that last night was the worst. Her daddy had used ugly words and even threatened her mommy with harm. Then he hit her, something he had never done before. This was what brought her reaction at lunchtime today.

"Daddy, that's why I asked you that question. I couldn't imagine our home without you, Daddy!" he said as sorrow filled his face and voice again.

I tried to explain that his mommy and I were very committed to the Lord Jesus Christ, and our marriage had been in His will and for His glory. I sought to show him that Christians look at marriage differently than those who do not know Christ. We seek to follow the Word of God in seeking a mate and setting up a marriage. I didn't want to give a deep theological lesson at this point, but only say enough to comfort him so he would be assured of the stability of his home.

I thought I had satisfied him till he said, "But, Daddy, April's father is a preacher too! Can real preachers do something like that? Can real Christians act like that? I thought real Christians were to be like Jesus? How can he do something like that and be a real Christian?"

Again it wasn't the time for a theology lesson. At this point I only wanted to settle his mind so he could rest easy that night and in the days ahead be able to encourage April.

I marveled at his spiritual sensitivity and insight. He was a very fine young son. He was obedient to his parents. He loved to study the Word of God. He was an avid reader of Christian books. He never gave any one trouble, but was cooperative in all things. He truly cared for others. He was loved by every one at Unity Baptist Church, the place he had grown up.

Several times previously he had amazed me with his spiritual language and understanding of theology. He knew that sin was against the holy God of heaven, and once I had found him crying because he had disobeyed God in something that seemed minor to most adults as well as children. He knew what repentance and faith were, and had professed faith in Christ as his Lord and Savior.

In fact, a father could not have asked for a better son. He was the apple of both his parents' eyes. I wondered sometimes what life had been before the Lord gave him to us, and what it would be like if God ever in his providence took him from us. Our experience with Dink's loss of a son had caused us to cherish young Ira in a deeper and more appreciative manner.[1]

He had one last question before he went back to sleep.

"I told April that you might be able to help her daddy. After all, you are both preachers! Preachers should be able to understand one another and talk to each other about things like these, shouldn't they? Will you help April's daddy?"

I didn't want to discourage him, and I was more than willing to try to see April and her father, and so I assured him of that. But at the same time, I knew that a preacher away from God could be like a bull in a rodeo ring---tough to tame and control. Usually such a man is out of fellowship with God, having acted in that manner because of other sin. And usually he did not want someone to remind him of his sin, since so often as a pastor, he had done a significant amount of marriage counseling.

I didn't know it, but many surprises were facing me before I was finished with this man---even a new journey!!

What's Your Daddy's Name?

I agreed to meet with April and Ira, Jr. the next day after school. My teaching schedule would allow me to get home just about the time they would get out of school. She didn't live too far from us, and we didn't live far from the school. They could walk to our house to meet with me, and then Ira could walk her home afterwards.

Terry, my wife, was dying to meet April, so after some pleasantries together as a family with her, my wife excused herself, and I was left with the two ten year olds. She immediately set forth the question.

"Mr. Pointer, will you help my daddy?"

Immediately with these words, she began to cry.

She was a cute little girl with a very sweet personality. I could understand why young Ira was drawn to her. She was open, innocent, very pretty, sincere, extremely polite (she used "sir" all the time), and she had a very disarming southern drawl (I will not try to communicate her drawl on these pages). She had big blue eyes and light colored hair.

When she started crying, both young Ira and I sought to calm her. I assured her that I would seek to help her father, but I needed an address where I could reach him. In answer to that request, she proved herself to be a very organized little girl, as she assured me she had it in her books, and started to reach to get it. I told her that it could wait. What I wanted right now was some information about her daddy. The following facts came forth in her response, which was sprinkled with moments of tears.

Her father had pastored in Georgia for the past ten years or so. That's where she had been born and had spent all of her life, until her daddy left the family. Then she and her mother moved back to Seminary City to be closer to family members. It seems her father was from Georgia, and her mother was from the Seminary City area. Her parents had met while he was attending Evangelistic Baptist Seminary. Since his days at Seminary City preceded my days as a student there, I figured I did not know him.

Her father's ministry in Georgia had seemed to be fruitful. He had taken an almost dead church, and built it into a church with about a thousand people attending. Her eyes lit up through her tears when she said, "Sir, you ought to hear my daddy preach!" But then the gloom came back with greater evidence, as she returned to speak of his fall.

She continued.

"Every thing was fine, as far as I knew, until one night I was awakened by the noise of mommy and daddy arguing. I was very frightened, so I got up out of bed and went to the top of the steps, so I could hear what they were saying. It was then that I heard daddy tell mommy that he didn't love her any more, and that he was going to leave her, so he could go live with Sarah Sankster, a lady in the church. Mommy was very upset and was crying. She told daddy to get out of the house now and never come back. Daddy said that was fine with him, because he had never loved mommy. He said he had only married her because I was going to be born."

She then looked at me with puzzled eyes.

"Sir, does that mean I wasn't wanted? And was I the reason they had to get married? And am I the reason that they aren't together today?"

She began to cry with brokenness again.

I wondered how men, especially preachers, could be so cruel, thinking only of themselves and the satisfaction of their own lusts, while doing something like this. How could they forget vows spoken before God? How could they hurt little girls like April and even little boys like Ira? How could they destroy their own ministries, which had seemed to have the blessings of God upon them? How could they be so blind to the multitudes they hurt in the churches they pastored? Yet, I reminded myself, is that not the nature of sin? What a testimony this was to the depravity of man's heart as well as the deceitfulness of sin itself. Men will follow sin and love sin even if it destroys not only the lives of others, but their own lives as well. What fools men are when it comes to their own lusts and pleasure!

I sought to assure April that she was born in accordance with the divine providence of God, regardless of the circumstances.

"Sir, what do you mean by the providence of God?" she asked.

To my surprise, young Ira spoke up here to ask if he could answer her question. I told him that he could surely help her here. I began to wonder about the difference of theology between myself and April's father.

"Providence means that God is in control of everything, and that all things happen like He has planned," young Ira answered. "That's what Ephesians 1:11 says!"

He added something which warmed my heart, even in the middle of this heartbreaking setting.

"April, though we cannot understand it nor explain it fully with our minds, the Bible plainly says in Romans 8:28 that our God is working all things together for good, especially for those who love Him and who are called according to His purpose."

It was then that I knew he had been listening to my sermons (I was the only pastor he had ever had---until now), and that he had given some thought to these matters.

"Does that mean," she asked young Ira (she was now talking to him, so I just listened) "that all the sadness we feel now has been sent of the Lord, and will be used of the Lord to do in this world and our lives what He wants?"

Young Ira assured her that was exactly what the Bible says---God is working ALL THINGS after the counsel of His own will.

That seemed to encourage her, and I figured I could step back in for some final information.

"April, I don't even know your last name, something I will need when I go to find your daddy," I stated.

"Sir, my name is April Showers!" she said bluntly.

"April Showers?" I asked, somewhat shocked.

"Yes sir, April Showers. Just like showers in April."

I could see that she could be as refreshing as showers in April, but the expression by itself was not what floored me.

"I had a friend named Showers years ago who said if God ever gave him a little girl, he was going to name her April Showers!" I noted. "Your daddy's name isn't Jasper Showers, is it?" I asked.

"Yes sir, Jasper Showers---that's my daddy!" she confirmed to my surprise.

"April, your father is the man who led me to the Lord Jesus years ago when we were back in high school!"

Who Was Jasper Showers?

After Ira, Jr. and April had left, I still was trying to get over the shock. The young man who had led me to Christ was April's father, and he was the one she was asking me to see and help. I went to our family room and sat down, and after pushing back in my chair, my mind recalled my memories of Jasper Showers.

I remembered the day I first met him. Though I had seen him from a distance, and though I knew he was one of those guys who called himself a "born again" Christian, I had never become the object of one of his "witnesses" for Christ. In fact, I kind of dodged him, not even willing to consider his Christian witness, because I thought he was kind of a radical personality.

The first day I really met him was when I was a freshman and he was a sophomore in high school. I found myself alone in the hall at my locker, when he stopped and cornered me with his friendly but forceful witness for Christ.

"Hey!" he greeted me. "How you doin'. Do you know Jesus?" he demanded with a big "good-old-boy" smile on his face.

"I'm fine, Jasper. How are you today?" I asked, trying to get him off my back, like a fighter pilot trying to shake an enemy plane. But he seemed to have a "gift" of dodging any decoy one sent up, while staying in the hunt.

"I'm saved, sanctified, livin' above sin, and strivin' to get in!" he shot back at me laughing. "How bout, you?"

I didn't know then, but his statement was an Arminian shibboleth, and all the phrases he used were packed full of theological meaning. The most loaded and revealing phrases were "livin' above sin" and "strivin' to get in." "Living above sin" meant one as a Christian could live a sinless life, and "striving to get in" referred to the idea that the Christian must strive all of his life to keep his salvation, lest he lose it, and miss entering the gates of heaven. But I didn't understand all of this then. As a lost man, I just saw Jasper as a religious enthusiast, who seemed to enjoy getting on peoples' nerves. I never mistreated him, but just tried to peacefully co-exist with him and people like him.

But in the passing of time, we became close friends. After I dodged his witness successfully for awhile, he seemed to understand that the way to "convert" me was not to bombard me with his pious platitudes. In fact, he seemed to become an ordinary guy, instead of a Christian who gloried in getting people to dislike him (so it appeared to me). It's one thing to be faithful to Christ in our witness, and to suffer persecution for His glory. It's another thing to seek persecution for persecution's sake, rather than to suffer for true godly living.

I even came to enjoy his "Southern sayings," though at times he could be brutal with them. I remember the day he said of one of our teachers, that "She fell outta the ugly tree, an' hit every branch on her way down!" Or another time he said of a girl, who refused to date him that, "She was so stuck up, she'd drown in a rainstorm!" Of course he would always try to soften it with, "Bless her heart!!"

Thus in the next two years, until he graduated, we had a lot of good times. I tolerated him and he tolerated me, but there was a genuine respect for one another. I must confess that the Lord used Jasper's witness in my life. The Spirit of

God spoke to me through the Word of God that he gave me to read. Then came the night of my conversion. When I brought up the subject of my spiritual need, he was there to pray with me and to point me to Christ as the only Savior.

When Christ saved me that night, he exclaimed, "Hallelujah! I've been to three hangins,' a hog-killin,' and a county fair, an' I ain't never seen nothin' like this!! I thought you was runnin' from the Lord like a scalded dawg!!"

But after he graduated from high school, I lost track of him. I knew he went to Seminary City, and then I heard that he went to pastor a church in Georgia. But it seemed that after we parted company, neither one of us made any effort to contact the other.

I wondered, as I sat thinking, what his attitude would be towards me now? Maybe I should have sought to keep up with him. Would he still have the same happy-go-lucky attitude, along with his big smile? Would he still be speaking his Southern expressions? Would he (as one of his sayings said), "be as nervous as a long-tailed cat in a room full o' rocking chairs?"

I decided to take a trip to Georgia early the next Saturday morning (only a three-hour trip), and see if I could find him. I hoped he wouldn't be "as slick as an eel in a churn of hot butter."

Will You Let Me Help You?

That next Saturday morning, without giving Jasper any warning, I drove to Georgia to see if I could find him. I have discovered in the ministry that sometimes old friends who had strayed from the Lord, would run from you if they knew you were coming, if they had time to think about it. While on the other hand, they would talk with me if I came unexpectedly.

I had concluded that a warning about a preacher coming to see a professing Christian who has sinned, could give the person too much time to think about the visit, whereby the imagination would be stirred. Then because of the great guilt, they might think I was coming to jump all over them, and to chastise them with the most stringent and arrow-like language. But on the other hand, if I showed up unexpectedly, they could see immediately that I was coming in humility and with grace, though I was not coming to condone their sin.

I found the house where he and Sarah Sankster were living. I had never met her, so I hoped she would not be at home, as she might see me as a threat to her relationship with him. It was about nine o'clock in the morning, and I parked the car across the street from the house, and then just observed the area for about five or ten minutes. No one was going in or out, so I started towards the front door. Maybe they were still sleeping.

Taking a deep breath, I began to knock, first gently, and then, when there was no answer, a little more firmly with accompanying noise. I listened to see if there were any reciprocating noises from inside the house. I heard the door locks being unfastened, so I took a second deep breath. Then, as the door swung open, I found myself face to face with old Jasper himself. He was so shocked that he couldn't speak for a second, and he seemed puzzled as to what to do. Should he invite me in, or should he slam the door in my face?

I smiled a big smile, and beat him to the punch.

"Man, you look as purty as a speckled pup!" I offered, using one of his old Southern sayings. And with a shaking of my head, and with a big laugh, like we used to guffaw together, I checked him in his tracks with, "Now you ain't gonna take off on me like Moody's goose, are you?"

That broke the ice, letting him know I had come as a friend, though I would not condone his actions.

He answered my Southern sayings (ones I had gotten from him) with a couple of his own.

"Well, knock me down and steal muh teeth! You sure did jar my preserves this mornin'."

Then he did what I had hoped he would do.

"Let's us get outta here an' go down to the restrunt where we can talk. This place is like New York. Its got lots a' restrunts."

He got in my car, and directed me to a local "restrunt." I was surprised at how friendly he was, but then I hadn't broached the subject to him yet.

"You had any vittles today?" he asked.

"No, I haven't. I left Seminary City pretty early," I replied.

We sat down and ordered, and then he was as forward as always.

"Well, I guess you must wonder why this old dawg ain't out huntin' no more for the Lord," he offered.

"Yeah, I kind of wondered that!" I replied, thinking I might be able to follow his lead and give him enough rope to hang himself.

"Well, I done lost my salvation outta plain old ignernce!" he declared. "An that ain't all I lost. I lost my youngin, April. Have you met her?"

"Yes, I met her. She and young Ira are very good friends, and she is very sad about all that has taken place," I stated, hoping to bring some tenderness to his heart, which it did as some tears began to come into his eyes.

"Ain't she somethin'? She's as cute as a bag full of puppies!" he noted.

"Jasper, what happened, if I might ask?" I queried.

"Well, I just lost my salvation, that's all! I was like a one-eyed dog in a chicken coop! I didn't know I belonged on the porch of the house. I guess I just got too big for my britches, and fell into adultery, and I lost it, and that's all."

"And you don't think you can get your salvation back?" I asked. "I thought your view was that one could lose his salvation, but that he could get it back by being saved again, and even again, if necessary."

"Well, Ira, I used to think that, before I lost my salvation. But I have been readin' the Scripture, and have concluded once you lose it, there ain't no gettin' it back. That would be more impossible than tryin' to herd cats!"

"What Scripture do you have for that idea?" I asked.

"Oh, I been finden' a lot of Bible verses for that view, but let me give you one that will slap your old view, like my old one, so hard, that you'll never believe it any more."

He then quoted Hebrews 6:4-6:

4 For it is impossible for those who were once enlightened, and have tasted of the heavenly gift, and have been partakers of the Holy Spirit, 5 And have tasted the good word of God, and the powers of the age to come, 6 If they shall fall away, to renew them again unto repentance, seeing they crucify to themselves the Son of God afresh, and put him to an open shame.

He went on and wanted to explain the passage to me.

He was convinced he had done the following:

1. he had been once enlightened (with the truth)
2. he had tasted of the heavenly gift (of salvation)
3. he had been a partaker of the Holy Spirit
4. he had tasted the good word of God
5. he had tasted the powers of the age to come
6. he had fallen away
7. he had crucified the Son of God afresh
8. he had put Him to an open shame
9. therefore it is impossible to renew him again unto repentance

"That passage is chocked full of the truth, ain't it? Even a blind hog could find that acorn!" he asserted.

"Let me ask you a fundamental question, Jasper!" I challenged. "Do you really want the Lord? Or is this an excuse to ditch the Christian life, the ministry, your family, and all that you have held dear as truth for the past years? Are you happy in this wayward life? Or would the one-eyed dog really like to get back up on the porch?"

He dropped his head and stared at the food on his fork for a few minutes. Then he looked up and answered.

"Ira, I wish I could believe what you believe---that one cannot lose his salvation. My life right now is crazier than a run-over dog! You don't know what a sight you were for sore eyes today. You and me's like two peas in a pod, except for our theology. I just can't believe once God saves you, you can't lose your salvation. I know you've heard all the arguments, so I won't give them to you. But you will never convince me of 'once-saved-always-saved.' I've known too many who professed but went back to the old life. In fact, yer Baptist churches are full of them. They got saved one day, but now they're as lost as a goose in a hail storm."

"Jasper, will you meet with me once a week to study with me from the Bible? I will not try to force my view down your throat. I would only ask that you listen and let me explain what I am convinced the Bible teaches."

As he was thinking, I spoke again, in his own language.

"If you won't study with me, then according to your own view point, you ain't got no more chance than a kerosene cat wearing gasoline drawers in hell!"

He looked up with a smile, seeming to be surprised that I had remembered so many of his favorite sayings. To be honest, I hadn't thought of them in years, but I had listened to him spout them for two years plus in high school, and to my own surprise, they were still in my brain.

He agreed with my offer, and we decided to meet every Saturday morning for discussion of the subject of salvation. My only question now was where to begin in such a vast study with such a convinced Arminian.

But as we parted, he warned me he would be a tough nut to crack. But I knew the truth was his only hope!!

What Is Regeneration?

The next week flew by as quickly as any I could ever remember, and soon I was facing the first day of doctrinal discussion with Jasper. I had decided to begin our study with the doctrine of regeneration. Though I did not know what Jasper believed on this subject, I assumed he would probably see regeneration to be a relationship rather than something deeper and life changing.

We both arrived at the same time at a point halfway between our two cities so neither of us would bear the burden of the drive. A local pastor in that small village had agreed to let us use his office, since it was Saturday, and he would not be around.

I hoped somehow we would delete the "southern sayings" from our vocabulary, but I guess I should have expected at least one as we greeted one another.

"You'll have to pardon me, Ira. I feel about as friendly this mornin' as a snake. I've got to admit to you that the grass isn't as green on the other side of the fence as it appears to be! I guess I should have talked to a cow before jumping the fence."

I wasn't exactly sure what he was talking about, but I guessed it was his relationship with Sarah. Perhaps the time had come when reality had caught up concerning their lives together, as well as understanding what he had lost. I didn't reply to his statement, but began our discussion.

"Jasper, I would like for us to begin with the consideration of the doctrine of regeneration, that is the new birth. This doctrine is very central concerning what takes place at the time of salvation."

He agreed, and so I set forth the following outline concerning the new birth from John 3, and we went over it together point by point.

INTRODUCTION---The necessity of the new birth

Jesus said in John 3:7 *Marvel not that I say unto you, you must be born again.*

Jesus did not say

It would be nice to be born again

It would be helpful to be born again

It would be beneficial to be born again

It would be spiritually profitable to be born again

It is my hope that you be born again

It is my desire for you to be born again

Jesus clearly made the new birth a necessity

You <u>must</u> be born again!

You <u>must</u> be regenerated!

But that raises the question

What is regeneration or the new birth?

I   REGENERATION IS A BIRTH

A birth is the giving of life previously not existing

Thus the new birth is not

the remaking or making over of something old

the renewal of something already alive

the reformation of something slipping away

the revival of something dying

The new birth is as Louis Berkhof says
    the subconscious implanting
        of the principle
           of new spiritual life
              in the soul
        which effects an instantaneous change
           intellectually
           morally
           emotionally
           in the whole man
        which enables the sinner to respond
           in repentance and faith
           to the outward or public proclamation
              of the gospel
    (see L. Berkhof, *Systematic Theology, p. 468)*

This certainly agrees with II Corinthians 5:17
    Therefore, if any man be in Christ, he is a new
    creature (or creation); old things are passed
    away; behold, all things are become new.

II REGENERATION IS A SECOND OR A SPIRITUAL BIRTH

In this whole context there is a comparison between our
first birth and the second birth.

A. <u>The first birth is a natural birth and the second birth
is spiritual birth</u>.

    John 3:3 and 7
        a man has to be born again or from above

John 3:3-6
>   one must be born of water--the physical birth
>   one must be born of the Spirit--the spiritual birth

B. <u>That the second birth is a spiritual birth agrees with other passages of Scripture</u>

we were begotten by the word of truth
>   James 1:18

we were born of God
>   John 1:13

we were born of the incorruptible seed---the word
>   I Peter 1:23

see also
>   I John 2:29
>   I John 3:9
>   I John 4:7
>   I John 5:4
>   I John 5:18

III REGENERATION IS A MYSTERY TO MEN

John 3:8 says
>   The wind blows where it wills
>> and you can hear the sound of it
>   But you cannot tell
>> from whence it comes (its source)
>> nor wither it goes (its destination)
>   So is everyone who is born of the Spirit

CONCLUSION
     Putting all of the above together we can say
          that a Christian is one
               who has been moved upon by the Holy Spirit
                    in a manner which man cannot explain
               whereby a deep internal change has taken place
                    so that he is a new creation
                         through the imparting
                              of a new principle of life
                                   by the Holy Spirit of God
               whereby also one's outward life is changed
                    in a very noticeable and drastic manner

When I finished going over this material with Jasper, including all the verses noted, I signaled to him that it was his turn to speak.

"I'm going to need a few days to think about this! You've raised some thoughts and verses I need to examine in more detail."

We agreed to go more deeply into the discussion the next week at the same time and same place.

He closed our discussion with another of his sayings.

"Right now I'm as addled as one of them brainy Northern Yankee sociologists tryin' to figure out Southern culture."

We exchanged pleasantries, and said good bye. I prayed as I traveled home for God to impact his heart with the truth.

I looked forward to next week, but right now I had a date with a little girl named April, who I knew was waiting at my house to hear about her daddy's response to our study.

Do You Know Jasper Showers?

When I arrived at my home, sure enough, I found April and Ira, Jr. waiting for me. As I pulled into the driveway, they both came running out to meet me.

"How is my daddy?" April asked. "Is he coming back to Jesus and home to mommy and me? I've been praying for him, and Jesus is going to bring him back!! I know He will!!!"

After assuring her that the Lord will do His work in His time, I left them to themselves. I heard young Ira say as I was leaving them, "Let's go pray for your daddy now."

I thought to myself, "With prayer warriors like those two behind me (there's nothing like child-like faith), how can I fail!"

Being a Saturday, the day passed quickly. Then in the evening, I had another visitor. The famous "Dink" walked in the door (he never knocked any more). I welcomed him and quizzed him on his recent whereabouts.

"Where in the world have you been? I can't remember a time when it has been so long since I have seen you?"

He shined his unarming smile at me, and said, "I been awful busy, Preacha! An' I got some information bout someone ya might know!"

"Who's that I asked?"

"Do ya know a guy named Jasper Showers?"

I wondered how in the world Dink knew Jasper?

"Do I know Jasper Showers?" I asked for emphasis sake.

Dink didn't give me a chance to answer.

"Dat's what I said, Preacha. Is you'se getting' harda hearin'?"

Then he winked at me, and I knew he was kidding.

"Yes, I know him! But when and how did you meet him?" I asked.

"He's in deep, Preacha!" he responded.

"In deep? With whom?" I asked.

"Wid da law!" he offered.

"What for?" I said, as I saw he was playing his usual game---dragging out a story for emphasis sake.

"Fer murder!" he declared without blinking an eye!

"For murder!?" I exclaimed

"There ya go again, Preacha! Or is der an echo in dis room?" he joshed me again.

But this was not a time to josh!

"Dink, spit it out!" I said, as always when he led me too far down this path. "Give it to me straight and clear and in detail!"

"Well, Preacha, he's been livin' wid dis Sarah Sankster after he left his wife. I'se sure ya know all 'bout dat!"

I held my peace, but gave him another look.

"Dey found her dead dis afternoon in da house where dey's been livin'!" he finally revealed.

"How did she die?" I asked rather shocked.

"Somebody, and dey tink it was Jasper, bashed her head in," he continued. "A neighbor found her dis afternoon, after she saw Jasper run outa da house and peel off down da street. Dey's lookin fer him now."

Just then the phone rang. The voice on the line sounded scared to death.

"Ira? This is Jasper. The police are after me, and they're gonna slap me into the middle of next week!"

"What did you do, Jasper?" I asked.

"Nothin, Ira. They think I killed Sarah! Ain't you seen it on the TV? My picture and everything! My cause is about as lost as that old war of northern aggression against the South! I'm dancin' around tryin' to shake the police like a boy with a bumble-bee in his britches!"

I had to ask a very direct question here.

"Did you do it, Jasper?"

"Do what?" he asked in dismay.

"Did you kill Sarah?" I said with all seriousness.

"Hush yo' mouth, Ira! Don't talk like that! She mighta needed killin'! Things were in such a mess! But I didn't kill her!!!"

I could see we were getting no where, except learning some surface facts. I had to urge him to do the right thing.

"Jasper, turn yourself in! That's your only hope!" I urged.

"But, Ira, they'll put me away so deep, that someone will have to pump sunshine in!" he spoke with grief.

"That's better than our having to put you into a grave, where you'll be about as happy as a dead pig in the sunshine!" I said, using one of his sayings for emphasis.

I kept wondering how I was remembering all of his old sayings! But evidently it worked. It always helps to speak another's language. He agreed to meet me, as he was in Seminary City, if I would go with him to turn himself over to the police.

It looked like we would have a lot of time to study Scripture together now---in a jail somewhere, depending on where they kept him till the trial!

How Did I Ever Get into Such a Mess?

Jasper met me as arranged and we went together to the main police station in Seminary City. They took him, as expected, and put him in jail, as they waited for paper work to move him to Georgia. The worst question I faced was, what will I tell his wife and especially little April?

When I arrived home, I called Mrs. Showers (Shirley), and asked her if she had heard. She said she had gotten the news, but didn't know where Jasper was. I informed her that he was in jail in Seminary City. She asked if she could drop April off with us, and also wondered if I would tell her about her daddy, while she went to see Jasper.

April, when told of her daddy being in jail, was quite mature (as much so as a ten year old could be), and simply responded that it was because he had not obeyed Jesus. Maybe now, she said, he would turn back to the Lord, and let the Lord help him.

Later in the evening, I went back to the police station, and they allowed me to visit with him for a little while. I wasn't sure what mood Jasper would display, but I was ready to talk theology, if he would so desire.

After some discussion about his situation, and I learned that he didn't know much yet, I asked him if he had given our last study much thought? I suggested maybe it would help us to talk about it, not only that it could be a solution to his problem, but also it might help occupy his thoughts while in jail. When he failed to respond, but just sat staring at the wall, I pushed him further.

"Jasper, could you sum up our last study?"

He sat for a few moments saying nothing, which raised in my mind the question whether he would respond or not. Then he began to sum up very accurately our differences on the subject of regeneration..

"I have always been taught and believed that the new birth is not a real birth, but it is only a figure of speech."

"Then what is the meaning of the new birth according to your belief?" I asked, knowing how he would answer, but wanting him to express it for further discussion.

"As a figure of speech, it speaks of a holy relationship and not a spiritual birth!" he offered.

I jumped on that statement like stink on a skunk (pardon the southern expression).

"And that is why you believe you can lose your salvation. If it is only a relationship, then it could be lost. But if it is a spiritual birth in some sense, whereby God implants a new principle of life within you, which brings new life, then to lose your salvation would be very major. That is to say, this regeneration or implantation of new life would have to be reversed, if you lost your salvation. God would have to withdraw or reverse that spiritual birth or the work of regeneration. Carrying the idea of a birth to it's logical conclusion, understanding it's depth and power of life, is it not impossible to become unborn? I only ask you to read the verses we have cited and tell me what they teach---that the new birth is a holy relationship? Or is it a new implantation of life---that is a spiritual birth?"

He thought for a moment and replied.

"Then you are telling me that my view of regeneration is too shallow? That if regeneration is only a holy relationship, then one could lose that relationship. But if it is a spiritual birth, which changes a man at the center of his being, then it cannot be reversed any more than a physical birth could be reversed."

"Yes, in a sense that is what I am telling you!" I replied. "But even deeper," I continued, "I am asking you if that is what the Bible teaches in the verses cited in our first study. Is this what the Bible teaches? Or does the Bible teach that salvation is only a holy relationship with God?"

Jasper thought out loud drawing his conclusions.

"It also means that if I was born again, as you define the term, then I am still a child of God! And if the new birth is only a holy relationship, then I have lost my salvation. So the question really is: Does the new birth affect me externally through a relationship with God and then internally, or does the new birth affect me drastically internally by the implantation of a new principle of life and then affect me externally in my everyday life because of that internal change?"

"Yes!" I blurted out.

"And," he continued, "my view means that when I lost that external relationship, I lost my salvation and any internal influence, which came from the external relation. But your view means that even if one fails to manifest the external reality of the inward change by the new birth, he does not lose the reality of that new life within."

Again, I agreed and added.

"Yes, one can lose the external manifestation for a time, but because of the reality of the inward new birth being so deep and irreversible, the new life will be manifested in time. If it is not, that one has never been born again to begin with."

"Then according to my view," he continued, "I am now lost, even if I was truly saved before. I have lost my salvation. I am doomed for eternal hell right now.

According to your view, if I was truly saved before, I am now truly saved still, and in time I will again manifest that salvation."

With this he cried out, "Oh, what's the use. How did I ever get into such a mess! I'm so lost and there is no hope for me. My life is in such a mess; not even God could get me back into His light. If I were to die and go to hell right now, I deserve it! Ira, why don't you bow out and leave me alone. My life right now is as sorry as a two dollar watch."

With this he broke down and began to cry. Perhaps now he was so deep in the woods of sin that we would have to pump the sunshine back in, as he had stated. But for God to send sunshine in the darkest of places was not an impossibility. Not with a wife like Shirley and a daughter like April praying for him, and a true salvation by the transforming power of the Holy Spirit.

A child of God can go deep into sin, but one of the signs of true salvation is the misery of the heart and the chastisement of the Savior, Who chastens all of them that He loves (Hebrews 12:6). And there is no chastisement like the chastisement of our Lord, sent by His love and grace, and for our good, but purposed to make us sick of ourselves and of our sins.

It seemed to me that this described Jasper perfectly at this time. Pity the believer who thinks he can turn his back on his Lord, and enjoy sin! Or be without chastisement!

The Lord does chasten---them that He loves!

9

Have You Not Been Born Again?

I prayed with Jasper, and I promised to come back to visit the next day, seeing his incarceration was in Seminary City, and the next day was Sunday. I called to see when his wife wanted to visit, and made my plans around hers.

So after church and a quick lunch, I made my way to the jail. They were kind enough to let me see him for a few hours. Understandably he was still down in his spirit, but he was willing, even desirous, to talk.

He told me of his initial involvement with Sarah Sankster. She had been a member of his church, and appeared to be all he thought his wife Shirley was not---understanding, tender, sweet of spirit, loving, encouraging as she stroked his ego, interested in his trials and difficulties, so appreciative in recognition of his gifts, sacrificial, humble, self-effacing---the most spiritual girl he had ever met.

The way he put it further was typical of his language.

"Ira, you've heard opportunity knocks only once? Well, with Sarah, opportunity knocked an' kept on knockin' till temptation blew the door clear off the hinges! What a fool I was! But that's sin, ain't it, Ira!"

But he didn't stop there.

"Ira, I was so obsessed with that sweet-talkin-thing that I was like a man on white-lightnin'! I couldn't see that she was as mean as a junk-yard dawg!"

So after "foolin-around" (his phrase) with Sarah for several months in a sinful relationship, he decided he wanted her more than he wanted his ministry or his family, or as he put it, even the salvation of his soul. He ran off to live with Sarah, and got a job selling cars.

"How long did it take you to come to your senses about your sin?" I asked.

"Well, at first, I thought I had died and gone to heaven, with all her 'darlin this, and darlin that.' An I made great effurts to please her. But then after a month or so, one day she innerduced me to a guy she said was her new boy friend. She said she'd met him over at the Red Rooster Bar over a few beers! An' then all the sweetness was gone out of her like a run-over peach! I seen then that I'd been barkin' up the wrong tree!"

"Why didn't you go back to Shirley?" I asked.

"Well, I hate to admit it, Ira, but I was so convinced that I was lost and could never get back to God, that I got me another girl friend, too!"

"How did that happen?" I asked dumfoundedly.

"Well, that honky-tonk life brought me to imminent peril, as Sarah had got me to drinkin' again. I don't know if you know it, but I was quite a drinker before I got saved back in high school. An when ol' Sarah dumped me, I went to the drinkin' dawgs. I can't go back to Shirley and April, after all I've done, especially while I'm in this condition. And since I'm lost, and its impossible to renew me again to repentance, there don't seem to be no hope for me or them!"

It was at this point that I pulled out my study material, and suggested that we continue looking at the Word of God to seek to establish whether or not he had ever been saved. He agreed, but I could tell it was with great reluctance. Perhaps, it was in realization that what I was saying was his only hope, as slight as it appeared to be.

I pointed out to him what we had discussed previously concerning our differing views of salvation, as we had centered on regeneration. He believed that regeneration was no more than a relationship that had been severed, when he left his commitment to Christ. I believed that regeneration was a transformation of his whole being because of the implantation of a new spiritual principle of life within him. Because of the depth of the work of regeneration, it could never be reversed. If he had been truly saved, he was still saved, and needed to come back to the Lord in repentance of his sins.

I showed him several verses which established that the one who is truly saved will evidence it by a godly life:

I John 2:29 (my own translation)
If you know that God is righteous, you know also that anyone who is doing righteousness has been born of him.

The text declares
    We know that God is righteous.
    Therefore we know
        that anyone doing righteousness right now
            (a present tense participle)
        has been born of Him
            (a perfect indicative passive verb)
The explanation of the text
    The person living a continuous godly life now
        experienced in the past the new birth
    Because once one has been born again
        the principal of spiritual life
            will make itself known
                by godliness and righteousness

Jasper broke in at this point.

"Ira, you ain't helpin' me none on this verse! I ain't livin' righteous now, so therefore I must not have been born again. Is that what you're drivin' at?"

"Jasper, did you ever live a godly and righteous life?" I asked.

"Well, yeah! But so what?" he pled in defense.

"What do you think produced that godly life? What does the text say?" I returned.

"Well, I guess I lived a godly life because I had been born again." he countered. "But I ain't livin' a godly life now, so I ain't born again now! Ain't that what your text says?" he continued.

"That depends, you see, on how deep a work the new birth was! If it was only a relationship, then you are lost now. If it was a transformation of your being by the implantation of a principle of new life, then you are still born again. You just 'ain't' (I used one of his words) evidencing it at the moment! But you are still saved, if you were ever born again to begin with. And that's why you are so miserable now. A dog returns to his vomit, and loves it because he is still a dog. A lost man can make a profession of faith, and then return to sin and love it, because he never was saved. But when a saved man returns to his sin, he is miserable. And though he may think he is enjoying his sin for a moment, the time comes when the reality of his foolishness hits him square in the face. It is then that the fullness of the stupidity of his sin sets in, as well as does the conviction of sin, which adds to his misery."

He sat and thought for a moment.

"You are miserable, aren't you?" I argued. "You are full of conviction, are you not? I know you see the stupidity of your sin, because you just told me all about your sin and its misery. Remember that God chastens them that He loves, and makes them sick of their sin and themselves. But He does it for our good and His glory!"

"I wish I could believe that I was still saved, and I could come back to the Lord!" he said as if he were thinking out loud. "Ira, this goes against all I have ever been taught and believed!"

"Yes, but he question is, what does the Bible teach?"

I noted for him other verses which taught the same thing---that one who was born again shows it in his life, and I pled my case again, that he had shown the reality of the new birth in his life for years, and therefore he must have been born again. And if that was the case, he was still born again, and could come back to the Lord, no matter the depth of his despair and sin.

I shared another verse with him.

I John 3:9 (my own translation)
Everyone who has been born of God is not practicing a continual life-style of sin, because the seed of God is remaining in him, and he is not able to practice a continual life of sin, because he has been born of God.

I explained further that this verse is not speaking of living a sinless life, but of a continuous godly life as the evidence of salvation, because of the new birth. I pointed out that this is true because the seed of God (the work of regeneration) remains in us, and we cannot live such a continuing life-style of sin.

I argued again, that if he had been born again, and that it was clear to me he had, because of the evidence of a number of years of a godly life, the seed of God (the work of regeneration) was still within him. He had not lost his salvation, but could come back to the Lord in repentance of his sins, not to be saved again, but to be restored to the Lord.

I urged him to study on his own the following verses:

I John 4:7b
Anyone who loves
has been born of God
and knows God
I asked him if he loved God at one time
and was that not the proof
that he had experienced the new birth
and that if he had experienced the new birth
he still possessed the new birth
because of its transforming power

I John 5:1
Everyone believing that Jesus is the Christ
has been born of God
I asked him if he believed in Christ at one time
not just with head knowledge
but with a true Biblical faith
I told him again that if he had
that this faith was the result of the new birth
and that if he had been born again
he still possessed the salvation
which had come to him by faith
because he still possessed the new birth

I told him his faith may be weak and under testing
but nothing could reverse the work of the Spirit
which is called the new birth

I John 5:4
Everyone who has been born of God
is overcoming the world
and this is the victory
which overcomes the world
even our faith
I asked him if there was a time in his life
when he was overcoming the world
Was that not a sign he had been born again?
If so then he was still born again
because of the nature of the new birth
as it was a transforming work of God

When I had finished speaking, he said, "Ira, are you askin' me to go back on my raisin?"

"No, Jasper. I'm trying to get you out of the pig pen and into high cotton spiritually! The evidence is that you have been born again. Even Christians can sin grievously against God. Remember David? But when Christians sin grievously in this manner, God chastens them. That is your problem now! You are God's child! His hounds of heaven are in pursuit of you, and you cannot hide from them nor out run them. They have caught you already, and are tearing you apart. Why don't you fall on your knees and cry out to God now for forgiveness of your sins, and return to him today!"

I challenged him as I closed, saying, "Jasper, who knows what further chastisement you may spare yourself! If you've been born again, you can't get away from God!"

10

How Deep in Sin Are You?

After church that night, I received a call from Shirley Showers, that informed me that Jasper had refused to see her and April, when she sought to visit him during the day. She wondered if I knew the reason for this refusal. I could only guess that he was too ashamed of his actions, and still convinced that he was in an impossible spiritual situation, which would keep him from any return to Christ or change of his present life. I told her I would question him about it the next day when I visited.

Therefore, following the teaching of my classes on Monday, I made my way to the jail once again. I would have gone to see him anyway, because I wasn't sure how long he would be in Seminary City before they shipped him back to Georgia.

"I hear you wouldn't see your wife and little April, yesterday!" I began.

"I'm too ashamed, Ira," he stated hanging his head. "If things get any worse, I won't even want to see you. How can I face my sweet little girl, April. And what could I ever say to Shirley, the way I hurt her. Now I'm just like a bump on a log---doin' nuthin, goin' nowhere, but conspicuous about it for the world to see!"

"Well, are you ready to look at the Word of God again?" I asked.

"Yeah, I guess so!" he said rather reluctantly. "But can I set the subject today?"

"Sure, why not?" I agreed.

He thought for a moment and then spoke.

"What I want to know is where you get your idea that a believer can never lose his salvation? You've about got me convinced that regeneration is a very deep and powerful work of the Holy Spirit. And I must admit, if that is the case, it would be difficult to reverse such a work! But where are the verses which teach one cannot lose this salvation, even if I would agree with your view of regeneration?"

I was overjoyed, because that was exactly where I was headed! So I began pointing him to my first verse.

John 10:27-29

> *27 My sheep hear my voice, and I know them, and they follow me. 28 And I give unto them eternal life; and they shall never perish, neither shall any man pluck them out of my hand. 29 My Father who gave them to me, is greater than all, and no man is able to pluck them out of my Father's hand.*

I summarized the passage as follows:

Christ's sheep hear His voice
    when He calls them to Himself
Christ knows them and they follow Him
Christ gives to them eternal life
    they shall never perish
    they shall never be plucked out of His hand
God His Father who gave this people to Him
    is greater than all
    so that no one is able to pluck them out
        of the Father's hand

I made some further comments:
God the Father
He has a people
He gave them to the Son
Christ the Son
He calls this people unto Himself
The people of God are called to the Son
They are known by Christ
They hear Christ's voice when He calls
They come to Christ when He calls
They follow Christ when they come to Him
They shall never perish
a double negative in the Greek---οὐ μη
an emphatic negative which means
they shall never ever perish
under any circumstances
any time
any place
any where
They are absolutely secure
No one is able to pluck them
out of the hand of the Son
No one is able to pluck them
out of the hand of the Father

I stopped and observed his reaction, and then drove home my point.

"Is that not security? Eternal security? Absolute security? Impregnable security? For all who have truly experienced the new birth!"

I could have kept on preaching and emphasizing what the passage said, but it was so clear, who could miss it?

But when he just looked at the Bible in his hands as if dumfounded, I went to another verse.

"How about Philippians 1:6?" I asked.

Philippians 1:6
>*Being confident of this very thing, that he who has begun a good work in you will perform it until the day of Jesus Christ.*

I outlined the ideas of the verse again:
Paul has the confidence
 that God who has begun a good work
  in the Philippian believers
  will perform it to the day of Jesus Christ
 the good work seems clearly to be salvation
I continued in greater depth in outline further
 there is no condition in this statement
  that is no "if" clause
   if you continue in Christ
   if you do good works
   if you hang on to your salvation
   if you pray much
   if you don't fall from grace
   God will perform the good work begun
    in you
 there is nothing but the straight statement
  God will perform the good work in you
  till the day of the Lord Jesus
 the Greek word here for "perform" means
  to bring to an end
  to finish or to complete
  to perfect or carry out to completion
  (the word is a future indicative active)

> thus God regarding this good work of salvation
>> shall bring it to an end
>> shall finish it
>> shall complete it
>> shall perfect it
>> shall carry it out to completion

"Where is there any condition given to man?" I queried. "There are no ifs, ands or buts about it. Where is there any question of the outcome of God's work of salvation in a believer? Where is there any ground for your thinking that you have lost your salvation? Where is there any possibility of your regeneration being reversed and withdrawn?"

Again, he did not answer, so I continued by giving him several more verses.

Romans 8:35-39

> *35 What shall separate us from the love of Christ? Shall tribulation, distress, or persecution, or famine, or nakedness, or peril, or sword? 36 As it is written, For thy sake we are killed all the day long; we are accounted as sheep for the slaughter. 37 Nay, in all these things we are more than conquerors through him that loved us. 38 For I am persuaded that neither death, nor life, nor angels, nor principalities, nor powers, nor things present, nor things to come, 39 Nor height, nor depth, nor any other creation, shall be able to separate us from the love of God, which is in Christ Jesus our Lord.*

According to Paul
    the believer is under attack
        by tribulation
        by distress
        by persecution
        by famine
        by nakedness
        by peril
        by sword
    the believer is being killed all the day long
        the Greek verb---a present indicative passive
            continuous action of suffering death
                at the hand of another
        this clearly speaks of persecution
    the believers are seen as sheep for the slaughter
        constant pressure of suffering
        continual stress of persecution
    the question---will this separate us from Christ?
        from the love of Christ
    the answer is a strong persuasion of Paul
        that nothing or no one shall separate us
            from the love of God
            which is found in Christ Jesus
                not death
                nor life
                not angels (even fallen ones)
                not principalities
                not powers
                not things present
                not things to come
                not height
                not depth
                not any other creature or creation

I spoke again directly to Jasper.

"Is this not an undeniable statement of the believer's security in Christ? of the believer being kept by Christ? of no power, even Satan himself, being able to separate us from Christ?"

He still sat staring blankly at his Bible.

I didn't mean to pressure him, but I spoke again.

"Is this not an undeniable statement that Jasper Showers is secure in Christ? That you are kept by the power of Christ, and that not even Satan is able to separate you from the love of Christ?"

Finally he spoke!

"Ira, I'm sorry! I must admit that this sounds gooder'n grits, but I'm a lot deeper in sin than you know or could imagine! I just can't be a saved man! I don't doubt that I was saved! But there is no way I could be saved now!"

Then I heard the words I hoped I would never hear from him.

"Ira, just get out of here and leave me alone. I don't want to see you again---ever! If you want to do me a favor, leave me alone, and tell Shirley and little April to leave me alone too!! I never want to see any of you ever again!!" With that, he rose to his feet, called for the guards to take him back to his cell, and our conversation was ended.

I couldn't help but wonder what he meant when he said he was deeper in sin than I could imagine. In a few hours, I would understand quite well!

11

What Happened, Jasper?

As I drove home this sad night, I tried to imagine how Jasper could be in sin "deeper than I could imagine." When I got home, I called my expert on the depths of sin---the Dink man.

"Hey, Preacha, I didn't see ya at school today," he offered as he answered the phone. "Where ya been!"

I explained my day to him, and then asked, "Dink, have you got any connections down in Georgia?"

He knew why I was asking.

"You talkin' bout sometin' relatin' ta old Jasper?"

"Yep!" I agreed. "He said he was deep in sin down there? I wondered if it had anything to do with organized crime, or some get rich scheme, or whatever?"

"Let me look inta it, Preacha, an' I'll get back to ya!" he offered.

It wasn't long until the phone rang, and it was Dink again.

"Preacha, ol Jasper is in a mess fer sure!" he declared. "It seems he an' Sarah Sankster robbed an armored car of about five million dollars, and killed a guard in the process!"

"What? Are you sure?" I asked in unbelief.

"Well, dat's what dey claim!" he insisted.

"Huh! I won't believe it till he tells me." I asserted.

"Preacha, tell Jasper dat I'se got some connections down der in Georgia, and if I knew his full story, we might be able ta help him."

The next day was a Tuesday, and since I didn't have any classes in the morning, I made a bee line for the jail. I took Dink with me, in hopes that he might be able to get to Jasper, if I couldn't. Plus Dink might be able to help him with the trouble he was in, because of the connections he had in Georgia.

When I asked to see him, the jailer checked, and came back and reported he wouldn't see me. I asked if he would check again, only this time tell him that I know his problem, and I had a friend named Dink who might be able to help him. Evidently, it worked, because we were soon escorted to the visiting area of the jail, where Jasper was waiting for us.

I introduced him to Dink, but he said he felt like he knew him already.

When I asked why and how that was the case, he replied, "He's got a reputation!! I heard of him when I was in the pastorate and even of late. His reputation is that though he's a little fella in size, he's big enough to go bear huntin' with a switch. Don't mess with him!!"

Of course, Dink's buttons were about to pop, but I had to ask how he knew Dink.

"From every where! Preacher boys comin' back to Georgia from seminary! Prayer requests for him and his wife when his son was kidnapped![1] People who got saved from his witness, who came to our church! And just recently, through a mafia-type group known as the Almondine. It seems Sarah had some connections with that group, and knew Dink some years ago."

I stood there shocked!! Dink in the years since he had been saved from gang life among the Almondine, had become something of a celebrity, with a reputation that had spread far and wide. I was glad for that many times, and now even at this moment it had seemed to open the door for us to Jasper.

Dink took up the conversation very forcefully at this point. He was a take-charge kind of guy!!

"Jasper, ya need prayer, so let's pray for ya, before ya tell us what's goin' on here. We can't help ya unless ya come clean wid' us."

He then cut loose praying. He didn't care who heard, or who might criticize him. The world was shut out from his mind, when he talked with the Lord. And as he prayed, whoever heard got the gospel!!

When he had finished, he firmly told Jasper to tell us what had happened, whereby Jasper unfolded a story which was almost beyond belief.

I had already heard the part about Sarah appearing to be so much, and yet proving to be so little. How she led Jasper back into a life of sin, was as shocking and as sad as it was the first time he told me of it.

He paused for a moment of tears, and then Dink instructed him gently to get to the part about all the deep trouble "beyond imagination," and also about her death.

He told of several men meeting at their house, and planning with Sarah the robbery of the armored car. He was excluded from their plans, but they knew he had heard enough to scuttle the robbery, so they threatened him with death if he exposed them or tried to stop them. He was caught in the middle of it all, and was scared to death, and so he began to drink all the more. He spent a few weeks where he would go to work in the morning, and then drink himself to sleep at night, so he wouldn't have to think about the whole situation.

Finally the day of the robbery attempt came. He pled with Sarah not to go through with it, but she wouldn't listen. She and her friends tied him up, while they went to pull off the robbery. When they came back, they were quite shook up over something, and he could tell it hadn't gone quite right. But they did have the money, about five million dollars. They finally told him that they had to kill one of the guards, and that was confirmed later on television. They hid the money somewhere, but he was not sure exactly where. They were going to let things cool down before they split the loot.

When they all came under suspicion from the police, he seemed sure it was these guys who killed Sarah, and made off with the money. He was left to bear the blame for not only the robbery, but also for her murder. He had no alibi for the day of the robbery, because of the fact they had tied him up and he was absent from work. On the day of her murder, he was with me, but he didn't go straight home after we parted, so he had no alibi for that period of time when Sarah was murdered. Plus it was one of his tools that had killed her!! The police were still convinced that he knew where the money was hidden.

"Ira, do you see now why I didn't want to see Shirley or little April? They're so sweet and so innocent! How could I drag them through all of my sin and its results, and even that which is yet to come---maybe even a death sentence for murder!"

I assured him I understood, but that if what he told us was true, we would be on his side all the way, in trying to bring the guilty to justice.

Then I gave him a strong admonition!

"Come back to Jesus first, Jasper! It will make everything else easier, no matter how dark it looks now! You say you can't! But is it that you can't or you won't?"

12

What Is Justification by Faith?

I had expected the authorities to move Jasper back to Georgia, but some technicalities were holding it up. At least that's what I was told when I called the next day.

So again, when school was finished, Dink and I made our way to the jail, not sure whether Jasper would see us or not. I wanted to see him as much as possible, while he was still in our city. Once they moved him to Georgia, it would be quite a drive to talk to him.

He did agree to see us, and seemed to be in a better mood. I had asked Dink to do the talking, that is, if he would see us. I told Dink to be kind but firm! Sure enough, he was.

"Jasper, we ain't got much time, so why don't we study da Word of God together!" he stated forcefully. "Preacha, what's we gonna study today? I need sometin' from da Word!"

I had decided to set before Jasper the doctrine of justification by faith alone. So I began in the following manner.

"Jasper, I am positive you know very well the doctrine we are going to consider together today, that is, justification by faith alone. But I have found great blessing each time I meditate on this truth, and I thought it would help us all today."

He listened with an uncertain look on his face, so I continued.

"Now, through the history of the church there has been two major views concerning the subject. Let me define both views for our consideration."

I then presented the views in the following outline:

VIEW ONE---INFUSED GRACE

God infuses His grace into a man
    which enables a man to cooperate with God
        in order that he may be able to do good works
God accepts such a man on the basis of those good works
    which he has performed
        not by his own power
        but by the power of God working in him
Some call this justification by grace
    because it is the grace of God working in him
        which allows him to do such works
Others call this justification by works
    because God accepts such a man
        on the basis of his own good works
            even though they were produced
            by the grace of God
Thus according to this view justification is
    inward
    subjective
    experiential
    progressive---works must help produce it!
    uncertain---how many works must a man produce?

VIEW TWO---IMPUTED GRACE

Man is a sinner and could never produce any good works
    whereby he could be accepted by God

Man has no righteousness of his own
   therefore he is separated from God
Man in order to be restored to God
   must have a perfect righteousness
      which he does not have
      which he can never have by his own works
Thus man's situation looks hopeless
   due to a debt of sin which he cannot pay
   due to a required righteousness which he does not have
But Christ has a perfect righteousness
   and He made the perfect payment for sin
If man will look to Christ alone by faith alone
   God will place the righteousness of Christ
      to man's sinful account
         and man's sin debt will be paid in full
            on the basis of the righteousness of Christ
            not on the basis of anything man does
Thus according to this view justification is
   an instantaneous act of God and is not progressive
   objective not subjective
      it takes place at the throne of God
   non-experiental
      it takes place outside man's experience
   judicial
      it is a legal declaration at the throne of God
   by faith not works
      faith in the work of Christ not my works
      faith in the righteousness of Christ

I kept looking at Jasper, but could get no read on him. I was especially concerned where he was, in light of where I would now try to take our thinking.

"Let me draw one more conclusion from the doctrine as
we have presented it. Follow me carefully," I almost pled.
With that I gave a summary of what we had seen.

We have seen the following:
   Justification is by faith alone
      not by man's works
   Righteousness for us is provided by Christ alone
      not by man's righteousness
   Justification is at the throne of God
      not within the heart of man
         as regeneration is
   Justification does not change us
      regeneration is what changes us
         but acceptance with God
            is based on justification
               not on regeneration
   Justification gives standing in the presence of God
      based on the righteousness of Christ
   God declares us to be righteous
      though we are sinners
      for He sees only the righteousness of Christ
         not our sin
   Justification being by faith in Christ's work
      is irrevocable and irreversible
      is for eternity
   When God sees you or me now as His child
      He sees us clothed in the righteousness of Christ
         having been justified by faith alone
   Our sins can never condemn us again
      we are His children
      we are declared righteous before Him
      we are accepted by Him

> Who could ever possibly condemn us again?
> Eternally justified
> by the righteousness
> of Christ

I looked over at Dink, and I saw some tears in his eyes. And then he broke out singing:

> My sin, oh the bliss, of this glorious thought,
> My sin, not in part, but the whole!
> Is nailed to the cross, and I bear them no more!
> Praise the Lord, praise the Lord, oh my soul.

I wasn't sure his song spoke of justification, but it did speak of the work of Christ for us. He was totally oblivious to any one else around him. I noticed some tears also in Jasper's eyes, but not for long. He soon stiffened, as if he mentally was telling himself he would not break down in front of us.

I continued taking off on Dink's song.

"Jasper, if you were saved by faith those years ago, then your sins had been laid on Christ on the cross. Christ bore your sins in His own body. On the basis of His work and His righteousness, God declared that He accepted you the sinner. It was on the basis of the righteousness of Christ--- not on the basis of your righteousness. Do you not see that you might change and you might fail, but God's declaration based on His will from eternity and the work of His Son on the cross will not change nor will it fail?

"Could God declare you to be unrighteousness if He had declared you to be righteous on the basis of the perfect righteousness of His Son? Such could be possible only if the righteousness of Christ failed.

"But would it not be true, that God could declare you to be unrighteous, only if He had declared you to be righteous to begin with on the basis of your own works? But that would have required a perfection, which you do not have."

I decided to come at him from another direction, trusting God to use my words.

"Perhaps it was your own works you trusted all those years. Perhaps you were lost when I first met you back in high school, trusting the goodness you thought you had before a holy and righteous God. Maybe it was your works you gloried in all the days you spent in the ministry, and you cared not for the work of Christ. I don't know, Jasper, but I do know this. On the one hand, if you are lost, God will accept you by faith alone today as you cast yourself on the righteousness and work of the Lord Jesus Christ. On the other hand, if you have been saved, then you have not lost your salvation, for it was the grace of God that saved you, and it is the grace of God that keeps you, and the grace of God will bring you back, for you are still the child of God based on the doctrine of justification by faith alone!!!"

By now Dink was on his knees praying for Jasper. It was obvious that Jasper was giving all I had said full consideration! He could no longer hide his deep concern, and the moving of the Spirit of God upon his heart.

"Ira," he said, as he began with a sigh. "I always said the Lord didn't create anything without a purpose, but misquiters and flies. Now I have to add myself to that list! I am lower than either of those species of bugs! I don't know whether I'm a backslider or lost! I don't know whether I was saved and lost it, or never was saved! I am at wit's end corner, and there ain't no way out!!!"

With that, he walked out on us. I told him as he left that we loved him, and that God lives at wit's end corner!"

13

Could This Ever Get More Complicated?

As we drove home from the jail, I asked Dink if he knew why Jasper had not been extradited back to Georgia. He admitted that he did not know, and that Jasper didn't know yet either. His lawyer had told him there were some technicalities in moving him. Well, the next day those technicalities became a mountain of more grief for Jasper.

I learned of the matter as I was in my office getting ready for my last class that afternoon. Dink came bursting in all out of breath, as if he had been running. It was obvious he was about to bust with information about Jasper.

"You'll never guess what's holdin' ol' Jasper in Seminary City now!" he declared between breaths.

I hated it when he began that way. From past experience, I knew that he knew something very important, and he might play the "hide-it-as-long-as-I-can game" with me. But today, the news was so overwhelming that he couldn't keep it in.

"Jasper is bein' kept in our state 'cause he's been accused of another murder right here in Seminary City!" he blurted out.

"No way!" I declared in unbelief. "Who could that be?"

"Well, I'm not postive if Jasper knows 'bout all of dis yet. I got it from one of my friends down at da state office. He found out 'bout it and called me!" he explained, without giving me the key information in the matter.

"Okay, but who is he supposed to have killed now?" I demanded to know.

"Well, dey found one of da guys involved in da armored car robbery dead out in da weeds in some field yesterday. Dey say da evidence points to Jasper as da killer!" he explained.

"But when did this happen? He's been in jail here in Seminary City!" I reminded Dink.

"Don't matter. Dey figure dat it happened 'bout a week ago before he was jailed. Somebody bludgeoned dis guy ta death, just like Sarah. Dey know from eye witnesses dat der was three people in da armored car robbery---two men and a woman. Dey tink it was Sarah, an' dis dead guy an' Jasper. Dey figure he killed dem two ta get da money!"

"But did they find the money?" I asked.

"Nope, only a few bills totalin' 'bout a few hundred dollars of da robbery money was on da dead guy, and dat's how dey know he was in on da robbery. Dey figure dat whoever killed Sarah and dis guy got da bulk of da money," he explained. "An' dey figure dat's Jasper!"

"But what evidence do they have?" I protested.

"Well, dey had da murder weapon (one a Jasper's hammers) at da scene of da crime, where Sarah was killed, wid Jasper's prints on it. And whoever committed da second killin' left da weapon, which was another heavy hammer, at da site where da body was dropped. An' it was also one a Jasper's hammers wid his finger prints all over it!"

To keep us from getting confused, I set up a time chart of the main events of the crimes of the past few weeks. I also included on the chart my contacts with Jasper during this period of time:

Saturday One
> My first meeting with Jasper in Georgia

Sunday One
> No contact between Jasper and me

Monday One
> No contact between Jasper and me

Tuesday One
> No contact between Jasper and me

Wednesday One
> No contact between Jasper and me

Thursday One
> The day the guy was killed
>> but no body was found.
>
> No contact between Jasper and me

Friday One
> No contact between Jasper and me

Saturday Two
> Jasper and I study together at halfway point
> Sarah was killed and her body was found
> Jasper's hammer with his prints is found
>> at the scene of the crime
>
> Money for the robbery is on her body
> Jasper contacts me in Seminary City
>> and turns himself into the police there

Sunday Two
> I visited Jasper in Seminary City jail

Monday Two
> I visited Jasper in Seminary City jail

Tuesday Two
> You and I visit Jasper in Seminary City jail

Wednesday Two
> You and I again visit Jasper in Seminary City jail

Thursday Two or Today
    Murdered man's body is found
    The man had been killed before Sarah's death
        though found after her body was found
    Another of Jasper's hammers is found
        with his prints
        at the place the body was found
    Some of the robbery money is on the body

So we have the following:
    two murders
    two of Jasper's hammers with his prints on them
    robbery money on each of the victims
Thus all of this points to Jasper
    the weapons point to him
    the prints point to him
    the robbery money ties them all together

But in all this mess, I couldn't help but see God's hand working in these events. It seemed that Jasper would be in Seminary City for awhile, as the courts worked out their problems. That meant God was giving us time for his basic spiritual problem to be faced, as he studied the Word of God with me.

Could it be that the God of providence, Who had orchestrated all these things, was going to deliver Jasper from all these problems and accusations?

But how, was the question that remained. And I had to admit as I thought of it, that it was not going to be easy sledding!

14

What Is Imputed Grace?

As soon as classes were over, Dink and I headed for the jail to see Jasper. We prayed as we traveled, that God would open his heart to see us. Much to our joy, he did, though he was still in a sour mood.

"Did you guys hear?" he asked.

"Yeah, we heard!" Dink answered.

"My mind's like concrete now---mixed up and thoroughly set! My case seems like its set in concrete too!" he mused.

"Make ya a deal!" Dink offered.

We hadn't discussed anything like this, so I wondered where Dink was going. What kind of offer could we make with Jasper?

"You study da Word of God wid us, and we'll try ta help find dis other guy in da robbery, who seems ta be da logical suspect in both murders. Dat is, if you didn't do it!"

"I gotta a lawyer, Dink. I don't need you guys!" he stated with an adamant coldness. "And I don't need the Word of God!"

Dink called his bluff, when he stated in a matter-of-fact tone of voice, "Okay, Preacha! Let's us get outta here!"

He got up, and started to walk out, and I was forced to follow. But, I must admit, I was uncertain of this bold move.

As we moved away from Jasper, Dink spoke over his shoulder.

"You may have a lawyer, but I bet he don't have no connections wid da Almondine, da group Sarah an' dose boys wid her were runnin' wid earlier. If you ever wants ta get outta dis, you'se may have ta deal wid dem! Does ya know anybody dat knows dem?" he concluded, as we kept walking.

He let us walk out, and I wasn't too happy and let Dink know it, when we were out of earshot of Jasper.

"Dink, what are you doing? We just closed the door to any opportunity to help him!"

"Be patient, Preacha!" he admonished. "Does you want ta go through dis sour mood ever' time we visit him? You wait and see! He'll call us before da day is over, askin' us ta come back! Trust me!"

I guess maybe I just didn't have any street smarts or street courage, whatever it was, whereby I could bluff anyone! I had Dink bathe this move with prayer as we drove back to school. But Dink proved to be right. Later that evening, Jasper called me and apologized for his attitude, and asked us to come back. He was ready to take us up on Dink's deal.

The next afternoon, after classes again, Dink and I made our way back to the jail. Jasper came out, and though he wasn't Mr. Happiness, which was understandable, he still had a much more cooperative spirit. We talked for about thirty minutes concerning what Dink would do to seek to find the other man involved in the robbery---the man who was probably guilty of both murders.

Then we turned to our study. Jasper even spoke first.

"Ira, you set forth the other day the two views of justification, that is, infused grace and imputed grace. I know your purpose was to explain the two views. Could you show me today where the view of imputed grace is in the Scriptures?"

God's providence again was evident. That, in fact, was the preparation I had made for this hour. I pointed him to Romans 4 as the passage we would consider today.

Verse 1
>Paul asks how Abraham was justified
>>Or how was he accepted as righteous before God?

Verse 2
>Paul declares that if Abraham was justified by works
>>then he has a right to boast
>>>but it would be a boast of himself and works
>>>>not a glorying and boasting in God

Verse 3
>Paul asks, "What does the Scripture say?"
>Scripture says Abraham believed God
>>and his faith was accounted or reckoned to him
>>>for righteousness
>The word for account or reckon is λογιζομαι
>>meaning
>>>to impute
>>>to set down as a matter of account
>>>to credit to a person's account
>Thus Abraham's faith
>>was credited to him before God
>>for righteousness---something he did not have

Verse 4
>The reward is not accounted (λογιζομαι)
>>by grace to one who is working to receive it
>>for that would make salvation not by grace
>>>but something God owed him
>>>and something he had earned

Verse 5
>But salvation comes not to the one working
>>but to the one who believes
>>>on the One Who justifies the ungodly
>>>on the One Who accepts the ungodly
>>whereby the faith of that one
>>>is reckoned (λογιζομαι) to him
>>>>for righteousness

I paused for a moment, asking him, "Could it be any clearer?" I summarized the material as follows:

>Salvation comes by grace through faith not works
>>this is the way Abraham was saved or justified
>>this excludes works as the basis of salvation
>>this excludes faith and works combined
>>>as the basis of salvation
>>this excludes grace and works combined
>>>as the basis of salvation
>>this salvation by grace and faith not works
>>>gives the glory to God
>>>excludes man having any basis to glory
>>>>in himself or his works
>>this means salvation can never be
>>>something God owes a man
>>>some debt God has to pay a man
>>this means salvation is completely
>>>by the grace of God
>>>through faith alone in the work of Christ alone
>>this means justification is
>>>by the imputation of the righteousness of Christ
>>>>to our backward sinful account
>>>>at the throne of God

not by our mixing of our works with His grace
     so that we can do good works
     which results in God accepting us
Finally such a work of God is by pure grace
     grace alone through faith alone in Christ alone
       not being based on man's works in any way
    can never be taken away from a man
    will never be taken away from a man
    because it was never based on his works
       works didn't bring salvation to him
       failure to keep working cannot take it from him
The mighty and glorious grace of God that saves him
    will also keep him
    and will fulfill the work God has begun in him

I looked at Jasper, and asked him boldly if he had any questions.

He replied sarcastically, "If that's true, then he ain't doin' a very good job of keepin' me!"

"Jasper, do you remember your saying that people are funny, in that, they want the front of the bus, the middle of the road, and the back of the church? What does that statement say?" I challenged him.

"I don't know! I just use those sayins.' I don't analyze them theologically!"

"Then let me tell you what it means. It means man's problem is not God, but that man is proud and puffed up, and centered upon himself, like you are right now!"

We parted under some tension. But I was certain that God was working in some manner. Sometimes men have to get mad before they can get glad.

I was glad Dink had made the deal. That almost guaranteed he would at least see us again!

15

What Is the Place of Works in Salvation?

I must say, I was glad when the next day came. It was Friday, and we had decided not to see Jasper again till Saturday. That would give us and him a break of sorts, as the week had been quite busy. And though Jasper didn't seem to appreciate our help, we had to continue the work by faith, if for no other reason, than for his wife's sake and for little April's sake.

That evening Terry and I had Shirley and April over for supper, and I very delicately shared with them the events of the week, since Jasper would not see them. I was able to communicate more of the details of the whole mess, after Ira and April left the table to go pray for Jasper. It sounds strange doesn't it. I didn't say to go play, but to go pray!

Shirley was appreciative of the help we were trying to give Jasper both spiritually and legally. I wasn't quite sure what Dink had done or was going to do. Sometimes he carried these matters pretty close to his vest.

I was shocked to the core, however, when Ira and April came back in to discuss the matter.

April asked, "What's it going to take to break my daddy's heart, and bring him back to the Lord? Ira and I have been praying that whatever it takes, God will do it!"

"Whoa!" I thought to myself. "That could be pretty drastic!" I mused to myself once again.

"Is there anything wrong with that, Mr. Pointer?" she asked.

Evidently this talk deeply bothered her mother, as she saw some implications she did not like.

"April, stop that kind of talk!" she scolded. "God wouldn't do anything like that! So, stop that nonsense!"

I didn't know whether to say something or keep still. I wanted to tell her that God can do anything He wishes. He is not to be brought before the bar of our puny limited knowledge. He is not to be restricted by what we think is best for us. And we should be willing to do anything for His glory. I really wasn't sure I was doing the right thing in remaining silent. But Shirley had been through so much, and was till under severe pressure, that I decided not to deal with it at this time. Its kind of tough to teach a whole system of theology in one night---a system that one should have been learning for years. Yet still, I had mixed emotions about my silence.

On Saturday, Dink and I went to the jail once again to see Jasper. He seemed to be in better spirits, but still there was an edge in our relation with him. Dink filled him in on what he had done thus far in making some contacts in his behalf, but reported that nothing had turned up so far.

Then we turned to our study together. I had anticipated some questions, which might have surfaced in his thinking, concerning the place of works in the Christian life. If they have nothing to do with salvation, then where do they fit in God's scheme? Further, were we saying that one can be saved and then live any way he wants to live? Would we not be encouraging licentious living, if that were the case?

When I mentioned those questions, he agreed that I had anticipated correctly. So I asked him to turn with me to James 2 in his Bible. We read the passage together.

14 What does it profit, my brethren, though a man say he has faith, and has not works? Can faith save him? 15 If a brother or sister be naked, and destitute of daily food, 16 And one of you say unto them, Depart in peace, be ye warmed and filled; notwithstanding, ye give them not those things which are needful to the body, what does it profit? 17 Even so, faith, if it has not works, is dead, being alone. 18 Yea, a man may say, Thou hast faith, and I have works; show me thy faith without thy works, and I will show thee my faith by my works. 19 Thou believest that there is one God; thou doest well. The demons also believe, and tremble. 20 But wilt thou know, O vain man, that faith without works is dead? Was not Abraham, our father, justified by works, when he had offered Isaac, his son, upon the altar? 22 Seest thou how faith wrought with his works, and by works was faith made perfect? 23 And the scripture was fulfilled which saith, Abraham believed God, and it was imputed unto him for righteousness; and he was called the friend of God. 24 Ye see, then, that by works a man is justified, and not by faith only. 25 In like manner also was not Rahab, the harlot, justified by works, when she had received the messengers, and has sent them out another way? 26 For as the body without the spirit is dead, so faith without works is dead also.

"Part of the problem," I began, "is that James seems to contradict the apostle Paul. They both use the same three key words (justification, faith and works). Some feel they contradict each other. Our discussion will center on a comparison of the use each makes of these three words."

I then passed out the following outline:

I PAUL'S DOCTRINE OF JUSTIFICATION

A. The problem that concerns Paul is the lack of man's righteousness before God

Romans
1:18   the wrath of God is revealed against man
1:32   the judgement of God is real
2:1   man is inexcusable before God
2:2   the judgment of God again
2:3   do men think they can escape judgment?
2:5   man is storing up wrath and judgment
2:8   God's indignation and wrath again
2:12   man shall perish in sin
2:16   God will judge the world someday
3:19   all are guilty before God

B. The solution to the problem of sin that concerns Paul is how man can have right standing before God (justification before God) (see Romans 4 which we have just covered)

Paul is concerned about a true faith
    which includes the mind
        man must hear and understand the truth
    which includes the emotions
        man must be convicted by the truth
    which concerns the volitional
        man must respond to the truth
        not that the will acts of its own power
        but as one is enabled by God's power
            to cast oneself on the truth of God
            as a convicted sinner

C. The solution also included justification before God apart from man's works

salvation apart from works <u>means</u>
man cannot be saved by works
man cannot be saved by faith and works
salvation apart from works <u>does not mean</u>
one can possess true salvation without works
one can make works optional after salvation
salvation apart from works <u>also includes</u>
a true salvation will produce Christian works
a profession without works is false
a true faith precedes salvation
a true salvation will be followed by works
a true salvation will produce true works
the Biblical order is
salvation is by faith---works will follow
the Biblical order is not
works produce salvation
works plus faith results in salvation
faith/works brings salvation

D. A summary of Paul's doctrine of salvation

a. justification is before God
b. justification is by faith alone
c. justification is by faith apart from works

II JAMES' DOCTRINE OF JUSTIFICATION

If we take Paul's definitions of these three words
justification---faith---works

If we place Paul's definitions on James
    we will have a contradiction
We must see how James uses these three words
    we must not force Paul's definitions on James

A. James is concerned with a justification or
    declaration of righteousness before man

    Abraham was justified by works <u>before man</u> 21
        we are told that Abraham our father
            was declared to be righteous by works
                when he had offered Isaac his son
    Go back and study the life of Abraham
        he made a great step of faith
            when he came to Canaan
        he had a true faith though there were failures
            Gen 12 he went to Egypt—lack of faith
            Gen 12 he lied in Egypt---lack of faith
            Gen 16 he had Ishmael---lack of faith
            Gen 17 he laughed at God--lack of faith
            Gen 20 he lapsed at Gerar--lack of faith
        he finally evidenced the reality of true faith
            when he offered Isaac
            for all the world to see
        he thus was declared to be a righteous man
            not before God
                that had already taken place
                    see Romans 4 also
            but before men by his works
        his faith at this moment came to its fullness

22 Do you see how faith wrought with his works, and by works was faith made perfect.

a better translation of "made perfect"
    by works faith was
        consummated
        brought to its goal
        brought to its fullness
        brought to its full culmination
        brought to its end
thus James is not saying Abraham was saved
    by works
rather James is saying
    that Abraham's saving faith
        was brought to the God-intended end
            as it produced Christian works
thus God does not save us just to save us
    but He has a final intent
        that we live godly lives
            of Christian works
            for his glory
this is the concern of James
    (it is the same in verse 25 also---Rahab)

B. James is concerned with a false faith which is only mental assent

he uses the word "faith" to speak of both
    the true faith and the false faith

    only by analysis of the context
        can we tell when he speaks of each

he speaks of the false faith in verse 19
>*Thou believest that there is one God;*
>*Thou doest well;*
>*The demons believe and tremble*

he obviously speaks of a false faith here
    the demons
        have a mental knowledge of God
        have an emotional reaction to God
        have not the volitional response
            there is no surrender to God
    a false faith could have
        knowledge alone
        emotions alone
        knowledge and emotions
        even a false volitional response
            for a false reason
            but lack surrender
        but without all three it is a false faith

C. James is concerned with works as the true proof of one's faith

James speaks of true Christian works
    not law works to gain salvation
    not legal works to earn salvation
    but true Christian works
        produced by a true faith
    thus any works of man
        which proceed from any other basis
            than the basis of true saving faith
            are false works
James is clear in his statement of this truth

14 What does it profit, my brethren, though a man say he has faith, and have not works (true Christian works)?

17 Even so faith, if it has not works (true Christian works) is dead being alone.

18 I will show you my faith by my works (true Christian works).

20 But will you know, O vain man, that faith without works (true Christian works) is dead.

21 Was not Abraham our father justified by works (true Christian works), when he had offered Isaac his son upon the altar?

22 See how faith wrought with his works (true Christian works), and by works (true Christian works) was faith brought to its end.

24 You see then how that by works (true Christian works) a man is justified (declared to be righteous before men), and not by faith only.

25 Likewise also was not Rahab the harlot justified (declared to be righteous before men) by works (true Christian works), when she had received the messengers, and had sent them out another way?

> *26 For as the body without the spirit is dead, so faith without works (true Christian works) is dead also.*

I put together a final chart which compared Paul and James' use of these three key words..

WORD	PAUL	JAMES
Justification	before God	before man
Faith	true faith	true and false
Works	of the law to gain merit before God	true Christian works as the evidence of true salvation

My conclusions were as follows:

1. A profession of faith is only shown to be a true faith as true Christian works follow.

2. A profession of faith is questionable if it does not result in true Christian works.

Jasper was ready to jump in as soon as I finished.
"Where does that leave me?" he asked.
"It leaves you either saved or lost, depending on whether you were saved or lost to begin with!" I declared.
"Was there the presence of true Christian works following

your initial profession of faith? Forget about where you are now! What about those many years after you professed faith in Christ! Was there the presence of true Christian works, or were those works of the law, whereby you were seeking to earn your salvation?" I challenged him.

Silence followed my words to him, so I continued.

"If there was the presence of true Christian works, then you were initially saved. And in light of the doctrine of regeneration and justification, you are still saved now. But if there were no true Christian works, but only law works to earn salvation, then you were lost then and you are lost now---you have never been saved. Or even if you mixed faith and works as a way of salvation, you were lost then and you are lost now. These are the issues you must wrestle with and the questions you must answer!"

We had stayed too long, and our discussion time was clearly over. We prayed with Jasper, and then dismissed ourselves.

His parting words were, "I am a hopeless case. I think I'll just let them put me in the chair and fry me to a crispy critter. No defense. No lawyer. No theology. No God. No preachers. No family. No hope. No heaven. No hell. You can't get any worse off than that, can you? Maybe I'm an apostate, whatever that is! Or a reprobate! Cancel the deal, guys. I'm gonna bust hell wide open, if there is such a place, and you nor anyone else can stop me!"

"Not even God?" I asked.

"Not even God!!!" he replied. "Not even God!!!!!"

16

What Great Comfort Is His Providence?

On the way home that night, I expressed to Dink my deep concern for Jasper. I was really beginning to doubt if he had ever been truly saved.

"Dink, what about the deal. Is it off?" I asked him.

"Nah! He's so discombooberated in his tinkin' he don't know what he's talkin' bout," he declared. "He'll change his mind by tomorrow!"

The next day, being Sunday, found me worshipping with my family in our new home church, Grace Baptist Church. I must admit it was a little strange to listen to someone else preach, when I had pastored all those years. Young Ira was a little antsy, because he couldn't find April. They sat together every Sunday.

"Daddy, that's not like April to neglect calling me if she isn't going to be here!" he whispered to me with some concern.

"Well, maybe they got tied up with something. She'll probably be here soon!" I whispered back.

As the service continued, I was just getting into Pastor Bo Hayden's excellent message, when one of the ushers called me out of the service.

"There's been an accident!" he said, when we finally reached the vestibule of the church.

"Who? Who was in the accident?" I asked, thinking it might be Terry and little Beth, who had gone home after Sunday School because Beth had taken sick.

"My wife and Beth?" I asked.

"No, Shirley Showers and April!" he informed me.

"How bad was it?" I pressed him, as I began walking to the door to go somewhere. I didn't realize I needed to wait to find out where they were, I was so concerned.

"I don't know how bad the wreck was. All I know is they are at Memorial Hospital!" he stated as I shot out the door.

By that time Dink and young Ira were there with me. Dink had followed me out, when he saw me leave, thinking it might be an emergency. And while I was getting further information out of the usher, he had gone back in for Ira, Jr. I wasn't certain it was a good idea for him to go with us, but I didn't have time to make a case for either side of the argument. Besides, Ira, Jr. was a spiritual young man, and I trusted he could take what was ahead. Plus, I knew he would never stay behind, if it concerned April. He would have walked to the hospital, if he had to, not out of disobedience to me, but because of a compassionate heart.

As we crossed the railroad tracks, I saw a car upside down, broken in half, and smashed beyond recognition. Dink and Ira, Jr. saw it too.

"Daddy, that's April and her mommy's car!!!" Ira, Jr. exclaimed. "Oh, Daddy, let's pray!"

He didn't wait for me or Dink to pray. He began to cry out to God for his little friend, April and her mother. It was a submissive prayer, and a powerful prayer, recognizing God's sovereignty over all things, but nonetheless, asking for their protection and strength. Then Dink prayed, and by the time he finished, we were at the hospital. My concern was whether April and her mother were still alive! From the looks of the car, no one possibly could have come out alive in that wreck! Except by the grace of God!!! We would know very soon!

All three of us were out of the car, almost before it stopped rolling. Then it was a dash to the emergency door of the hospital. Not hardly slowing down, except to allow the sliding doors to open, we shot into the hospital, and rushed over to the first desk we could find with someone who looked official.

"Ma'am, did they just bring in a mother and daughter, who had been in a wreck, named Shirley and April Showers?" I asked in a voice twice the normal speed, and in the most serious tone possible.

"Yes, are you related to them?" the nurse asked.

I didn't care to give anybody's life history, but I knew the question was necessary and valid, so I explained to the lady that the husband of this family was in jail, and they had no close relatives in the area, and I was a very close friend. I thought surely that will suffice, but I had been shocked several times by some strange hospital rules.

"How are they?" I asked again.

"The doctor will tell you that!" she said.

"Where's the doctor?" I asked, no doubt showing some impatience by now.

"Just have a seat over there, and he will be out in a little while!" she answered again.

"Look, does it make any difference if I am a minister of the gospel?" I asked, not wanting to pull rank, but very concerned in light of the mangled car.

"No, even a minister would have to wait just now!" she countered, as I began to perceive a little sharp edge in her attitude and speech.

"Excuse me, ma'am, but we are very concerned, mainly because we saw their car and how badly it was smashed, and we wondered if they were still alive? Could you tell us that much?" I pled.

"They were both alive when they arrived here, and the doctor is with them now. The doctor will have to tell you any thing else which has transpired since their arrival!" she spoke, hoping to justify her reluctance to divulge anything.

I went and sat down, and realized that the nurse probably didn't know very much. I noticed young Ira slowly and inconspicuously making his way back to the desk. Maybe he would do better with the nurse than I had done. If not, I thought with amusement, we'll turn "the Dink" loose on her! But in all seriousness, I told myself that she had a job to do, and probably had acted as she was assigned in such emergency cases. What good could we do, anyway, going back into the emergency room? In fact, we might do more harm than good until they are ready for visitors! I reminded myself of something I have to remember always---God's sovereignty and providence. Then I sat as patiently as I could, except to get up once and call Terry, my wife.

As I sat down to wait again, my mind turned to two persons, Jasper and young Ira. How would they react, if death were involved in this accident? I remembered Jasper's words that not even God could keep him from busting hell wide open! And I also remembered Ira and April's prayer that God would do whatever it took to break her daddy's heart and bring him to Jesus!

Finally the doctor came through the door, walked toward us! We all stood there with our hearts in our throats.

It was another one of those major moments of life, when one could rest only in the providence of our great God, whatever the doctor might say. God is the one working all things after the counsel of His own will!

17

Can You Ever Forgive Me?

After a few explanatory remarks concerning who we were, and where the husband and father was, in order to satisfy the doctor as to our legitimacy as recipients of information concerning April and Shirley, we finally were given the desired information.

"They're both still alive," the doctor offered rather matter-of-factly, "but they're not out of trouble yet. We almost lost them both. The little girl is in a coma, and we don't know when she will regain consciousness."

"But they are still both alive?" I asked just to be sure I hadn't missed the doctor's point.

"Barely!" he confirmed. "If the father and husband is in jail, who will take the responsibility of telling him?" he asked. "Does he have a minister?"

"No, but we're both ministers," I noted. "We'll go and see him right now!"

When the doctor was gone, I told Ira that we would drop him by home on our way to the jail. His answer was strong and clear.

"No, Daddy. I want to stay here with April!" he said with tears in his eyes.

"But you can't see her, and maybe you won't be able to see her for hours or for several days!" I argued.

"Please, Daddy, let me stay. When you come back to pick me up, maybe we can see her then!" he urged.

In some ways it was one of the craziest things I could imagine---a ten year old kid sitting in a hospital emergency waiting room by himself for several hours. Even the hospital would probably have some objections to that!

"What will you tell someone who asks if you are here all alone?" I quizzed him.

"I'll tell them that I have a very good friend here in the hospital, and I am waiting for my daddy to come by and take me home," he said without a hitch.

Finally, I agreed with instructions for him to call mommy at home, if he needed anything at all or ran into any trouble. Having settled that, Dink and I headed for the jail, wondering what attitude we would find there today, and how it would change when we gave Jasper this latest news.

As we expected, Jasper refused to see us at our first request, probably still miffed at us from the previous day. When we shared with the jail officials the condition of his wife and child, they told him he had to see us, but they did not tell him why. He came into the visiting room with steam coming out of both ears and his mouth.

He swore at us a couple of times and then added, "If I could get away with it, I'd slap you two buzzards so hard, your clothes would be out of style when you woke up! Maybe I'll remember to do it when I get out of here."

"Jasper, there's someone else you need to worry about waking up!" I said hoping to jar him to listen to us.

"I don't know about anybody who's asleep, except maybe you guys and your theology which fails to see how lost I am!" he snarled with greater bitterness.

I wasn't getting anywhere this way, so I just gave him the news straight up.

"Jasper, you've got a daughter and a wife who are about to die! There was an accident, and April has not regained consciousness yet. Both are in critical condition at Memorial Hospital! The doctor says they aren't out of the woods yet! Any questions?"

I hated to be so blunt and to the point, but I saw no way to gently ease into the matter, in light of his foul mouth and attitude. I watched to see what his reaction would be.

He began to shout, "No, it can't be! No, it can't be! Say it isn't so! Please!"

Then he broke down completely. All the venom disappeared. All the arrogance was gone. He dropped on his knees and began to cry out to God for mercy for himself and for his wife and daughter. Though a grown man, he cried in the same manner as I had seen April cry when she told me of her daddy leaving her and her mother, and in the same way young Ira had cried, when asking if I would ever leave him, and mommy and little Beth. In an instant, God had broken him! And though the circumstances were sad, there was a victory gained in his soul.

Dink and I both knelt down beside him with an arm around him, and we wept too! I couldn't help but be convinced even more of the foolishness of sin! If Jasper had known where his straying would have ended, surely he would never have gone down that path, no matter how inviting it may have appeared. Yet the Word of God had warned him in so many ways---by admonitions, by stories, by commands. Yet sin is so inviting and deceiving that men sell their souls and future for it, only to be crushed and left dead in life and spirit because of it.

When Jasper finished praying, Dink and I prayed, thanking God for Jasper's prayer of repentance and reminding us all that God's providential ways are past our finding out. When we finished praying, and it must have been an hour that all of us agonized in prayer before the Lord, Jasper really did appear to be a different man.

"Can you guys ever forgive me for the way I have been actin'? I've been so stupid and you guys have been as patient and as smart as a tree full of owls. The wheels in my head have been runnin' but the hampster, he's been dead!"

He continued, giving more evidence of God's real working in his life.

"And by all means, tell Shirley I love her dearly! I'm so sorry for the mess I got us in. Ask her to forgive me. I will make it all up to her! With the Lord's help, we will defeat the enemy, and be back together soon. And Dink, the deal's on again! I do need and want your help! And Ira, I do want you to continue the Bible studies, and I promise I'll let the big dog eat and just listen and learn!"

I took that to be a promise he would be cooperative, and would join in the study with all his heart and soul. We left rejoicing, but mindful of how quickly things change in God's hands.

Two lives, which were completely healthy yesterday, are in much pain and hanging in the balance between life and death today, while another life, which was so full of rebellion yesterday is walking in submission to God today.

For a lost person or a weak Christian, such thoughts could be devastatingly frightful, but for the committed believer, the reality of a providential heavenly Father, who works all things after the counsel of His own will, it is the unbreakable anchor of his soul.

It is so sorrowful that so many men will not bow to God's person and power. They seem to want to relate to God only as His advisor, and when He asserts His Lordship and Authority over them, they get mad at Him because He refuses to go along with their plans. What blindness!!

18

Is It Ever Easy to Face Death?

When we arrived back at the hospital, I remembered that we hadn't had any lunch, and I had even forgotten to give Ira, Jr., any money for food. It was close to three o'clock in the afternoon, but of course, the situation at the hospital would dictate our next move. We found young Ira still sitting in the emergency waiting room.

I shared with him the Jasper's response to the news, and he lit up like a Christmas tree.

"Any word concerning April and her mother?" I asked him.

"Daddy, the doctor came out once about an hour ago and said April's mommy is better, but that April is still in a coma. He talked to me and told me everything. He even said I could see them when they were able to have visitors!"

I thought that sounded like a miracle! Young Ira must have talked to him like an adult, which he was so capable of doing. Or maybe the doctor saw the depth of his concern for April and her mother.

"Are you hungry?" I asked him, "Or have you forgotten what time it is?"

"I'm not hungry, Daddy. Besides we might miss the doctor coming out to tell us how they are. We don't want to miss that!" he assured me.

I didn't tell him, but after my years in the pastorate, hospital waits were unpredictable, including the length of time it took to get information.

"I thought you said we would go home, after I had seen Jasper?" I reminded him.

"Okay, Daddy. You win! But how will we know how they are doing! I think someone ought to be here to see and encourage them when they are able to have visitors. Who else is there but us?" he remonstrated gently.

"I'll stay, if you'se guys wants ta get some refreshment an food. If anyting major comes up, I'll call ya," Dink offered.

As it is so often the case, after we had set our plans, and as we were getting up to go, here came the doctor.

"Someone can see Mrs. Showers," he informed us. "But April is still unconscious!"

"You go, Preacha! You'se knows her best." Dink insisted.

"And you can bring the little guy, too!" the doctor said. "He's my buddy! He might bring Mrs. Showers more encouragement than all the rest of us! And he's more mature than most adults I meet!"

I smiled and nodded towards Ira, and he returned the smile. We followed the doctor to an emergency room, where a nurse directed us to Shirley's curtained area. It was obvious from all of the machines that her vital signs were being monitored.

Also, her eyes were closed, but I took her hand, and when she was aware of someone being present, she opened her eyes and nodded a faint hello. She saw young Ira, and nodded to him also.

"Shirley, we can't stay long," I whispered. "But in the midst of all of this bad news, I have some good news for you! Jasper has come back to the Lord. He wanted me to ask you to forgive him for all his sin against you and April, and he said to tell you that he loves you dearly! He says he is confident that God will defeat the enemy in this whole situation, and you all will be together as a family again someday."

She squeezed my hand and began to cry tears of joy, but then remembered the reality of possible bad news.

"How's April?" she said in a subdued voice.

I didn't know how much the doctor had told her, but I had to be honest with her.

"April is in a coma! But she's holding her own. We are praying and trusting God to raise her up in accordance with His will!" I informed her.

The tears continued, probably tears of sorrow now, mixing with her previous tears of joy.

I shared my thoughts with her in all honesty.

"Life is strange at times, and beyond our understanding. All of these matters are clearly unexplainable to us, but they are in the hands of our sovereign providential God!"

She shook her head in agreement, and knowing she was in need of rest, I suggested we pray before we left. I prayed, and was ready then to leave, but young Ira on his own began to pray also. When he was finished, there were tears in all our eyes!

Shirley gave us a smile, and said to me, "Ira, I hope you know what a fine son you have! It assures me to know that he is praying so faithfully for us, especially for April!"

On our way out, I asked the doctor if we could just look in on April. He agreed, as long as we just took a quick look. So we peeped through the crack of the curtain that enclosed her. We both cried again. It's never easy to face the reality of death itself, or even potential death, but it's even more difficult when death seems to be stalking one of such a young age!

19

Should a Christian Expect to Suffer?

There was no improvement in April's condition the rest of that first day. Shirley Showers was progressing well, while April was moved into the intensive care unit.

I wasn't able to get back to see Jasper until Monday afternoon, but then I was very encouraged with his spiritual condition. He was rejoicing over God's movement in his life, though he was very sorrowful concerning the sad results of his period of rebellion.

I asked him almost immediately if he had thought about whether or not he had been saved prior to yesterday. His answer was not unexpected.

"Ira, I've given a lot of thought and prayer to that question!" he stated. "Bless God, whatever happened yesterday in bringing me to the Lord was of the Lord and not of my power or ability. Try as I did, I couldn't defeat the enemy! If I was lost, I was powerless to help myself, as I was enslaved to sin! If I was just backslidden, I was equally helpless, in light of the way I had given myself over to the enemy."

"So what is your conclusion?" I asked again.

"Well, there are a couple of things that convince me that I was saved those years ago," he began to explain, "and that I did live the Christian life for another period of several years. But then it seems clear that I left the Lord and spent the past several months as a backslidden Christian."

"Oh, and what convinces you of that?" I asked.

He then listed the following:

1. He could not deny the misery of his heart and soul. A life of sin, that had looked so inviting and enjoyable at first, had brought the deepest misery of sorrow and conviction.

2. He could not deny the clear chastisement of God. There was no way he could call what had happened to his wife and daughter a mere coincidence. It was clearly the providence of God.

3. He could not, in all honesty, deny his original conversion. He had experienced true regeneration those years ago, as he was without doubt a new creation in Christ.

4. He could not deny the reality of a true Christian life with true Christian works during the years following his conversion. He was not a hypocrite. He was not working to be saved, but all his life was lived for the glory of God, and was flowing from the reality of Christ's power within him.

I smiled, as I stated, "The Bible studies we had with you were used of God, then, to help bring these convictions?"

"Without doubt!" he agreed. "The word came with power as we studied together. Why do you think I got so mean and nasty?---till God broke me! And He is the One Who moved with His power through the truth to break the control of sin over me!"

"Then you no longer believe a person can lose their salvation?" I asked.

"You are right!" he declared. "I no longer believe a person can lose their salvation, because of the very reasons you gave me from the Word of God! I want you to keep teachin' me the doctrine of salvation to clarify the other areas of that truth."

Remembering that neither of us had used any of his "Sayins," I chortled, "Ahm' fixin' ta do that!!!"

From the jail, I went to the hospital to check on Shirley and April. Shirley had been moved into a private room, though she faced a long period of recovery. April was still in the intensive care unit. I found Terry and young Ira visiting with Shirley when I arrived. It seems the doctor had given young Ira permission to visit when accompanied by an adult.

So, when we had visited with Shirley, Ira and I went to the ICU area, and peeped in on April. Her little face was so swollen with black and blue bruises, that we hardly recognized her, to say nothing of her other injuries. This seemed to be worse than the first day of the accident. Ira, Jr., had never seen anything like that, let alone involving someone he knew and cared for so much. I saw tears again coming down his cheeks.

"Daddy, I guess it's good that she's asleep through all this pain!" he stated, putting a good light on the situation.

"That's no doubt true!" I agreed. "Even if she was not in a coma, they would probably have her very heavily sedated, so that she would sleep most of the time any way."

"Daddy, how long do comas last?" he asked as he fought back more tears.

"That's difficult to answer," I replied. "Sometimes a day or so! Sometimes several weeks! Sometimes several months! Sometimes several years! It depends on the damage. Right now her head area is so bruised and swollen, it might be difficult even for a doctor to predict!"

With that, he declared matter of factly, "Daddy, Jesus is the great physician, isn't He?"

Not waiting for me to answer, he continued. "I like Dr. Sullivan, and I did pray for him last night, when I prayed for April. But I also prayed that Dr. Jesus would take over this case and do exceedingly and abundantly above all that Dr. Sullivan is able to do, and even above all we are able to ask or think!"

I marveled at his ability to mix difficult phrases of the Bible into his prayers and thoughts. Having stated the above, he reached out and took her hand and prayed for her.

On the way home he shared more of his young heart.

"Daddy, Jesus was a man of sorrows, wasn't He? If Jesus suffered, I guess even we as Christians can expect to suffer! And His sufferings were all according to the will of the Father, weren't they? If He, the perfect Son of God, suffered in order to fulfill His Father's will, I guess we as sinful men can expect to suffer also in order to fulfill our Father's will for us. To think we should not suffer, would be to think we are better than Jesus, and wiser than the Father. It's enough to know, isn't it Daddy, that our sovereign God is on the throne? It's enough to know that He rules our lives with love!"

Hearing nothing from me, he continued.

"But knowing that doesn't remove all the sorrow and tears, does it Daddy? Nor does it keep us sometimes from asking why, as long as we ask with a submissive heart!"

20

Are Trials Friends or Enemies?

The next morning, a Tuesday, Dink called while I was eating breakfast.

"Preacha, I won't be round seminary today, cause I'm goin' ta Georgia to see a guy 'bout da killins' and da robbery," he informed me.

"Have you discovered something over there?" I asked with understandable curiosity.

"Don't know," he admitted. "But dis guy called me, an wouldn't even identify himself, an said he wanted to see me 'bout Jasper's problem! So I don't know what I'm gettin' inta! He didn't even say why he wanted ta see me."

"Do you want me to go with you?" I offered.

"Nah! I can take care of dis okay!" he assured me.

"Well, let me hear from you immediately when you get back!" I instructed gently.

After school that day, I headed again to the jail. My schedule, it appeared, would be quite routine for the next few days. School, jail, hospital, and then home would make up my appointed rounds. After the jail, though, I would have to pick up Ira, Jr. to take him with me to see April. It appeared that Jasper would be in Seminary City for awhile, as the courts sorted out where he would be tried for murder first.

Jasper was in good spirits, and made a request as I began our time of study, though the seriousness of his situation had seemed to rob him of the desire to use his cute southern sayings.

"Ira, could we look at the plan of salvation as a whole? I ain't never got that all together, but I sense a need to do it now. Not that it'd make me any more saved, but it's just to clarify my mind on this whole subject of my salvation."

I smiled, and pulled out my notes, and handing him a copy, I stated, "Ain't that the berries? That'll be easier than sliden' off a greasy log backwards! That's exactly what I had planned for today!"

He was amused that I would use some of his sayings, when he didn't seem to be able to pull any of them up himself.

Listed on the notes were the key words of salvation and a very simple definition:

1. Conviction

    the work of the Holy Spirit to convince a man of his sin

2. Effectual Calling

    the work of the Holy Spirit whereby the elect are effectually called

3. Regeneration

    the work of the Holy Spirit whereby the elect are given a new principle of spiritual life

4. Repentance

    the work of the Holy Spirit whereby the elect have a change of mind, heart and will concerning sin

5. Saving Faith

    the gift of the Holy Spirit whereby

        a man casts himself on the Word of God

            concerning the person/work of Christ

            concerning the promise of the Word

            for salvation from sin

6. Justification

    the work of God whereby the sinner
        by grace through faith
            is declared to be righteous
                before the throne of God
                in a legal sense
                not in a literal sense

7. Sanctification

    a process wrought in the justified sinner
        whereby that individual
            becomes more and more like Christ
            in his character and life

8. Adoption

    the taking of one who is not a true son
        to be a true son
            with the position of a true son
            with the full rights of a true son
            with all the privileges of true son

9. Perseverance

    the fact and work of the Holy Spirit whereby
        those God has chosen from eternity past
        those God has regenerated
        those God has effectually called
    are kept by the power of God
        so they will never totally fall away
        so they will persevere in faith
        so they are and will be eternally saved

10. Glorification

    the work of the Holy Spirit whereby
        the elect of God are finally conformed
            to the image of Christ

After some discussion, I left with the promise that we would take each area separately in the coming days. I then scurried home, and found young Ira waiting for me, as he came bounding off of the porch as soon as he saw the car.

At the hospital things were about the same, though Shirley Showers seemed to be gaining slowly day by day. April was still in the coma, but they had moved her to a private room. Yet to be honest, I was beginning to be very concerned about her!

While we were there, Ira held her hand and talked to her as if she could hear him. Perhaps she could! Then, just before we left, he kissed her on the forehead, assuring her he would be back the next day, and we prayed for her.

On the way home, his thoughts tumbled out again.

"Daddy, trials and sorrows really are tough, aren't they. They are like visitors that we never would invite into our home, but here they come, nonetheless, and the time of their stay is not up to us. Uninvited guests, who sap the life out of a person, and never give an explanation as to why they are there! One feels enslaved to them. Yet they are sent of God for our good and His glory."

I nodded, and he continued.

"I guess our problem is that we look upon these sorrows and trials as enemies, and not as guests sent by God. Guests are to be welcomed, not shunned. So maybe the best way to treat these guests, though they are uninvited, is to welcome them and embrace them, and let them teach us as they will. If we fight against them, will we not defeat their purpose, and thwart the benefit they could bring?"

"You are right, son. Strange, isn't it? We don't welcome them, and we even cry when they come. Then we rejoice when they leave, even though they have taught us valuable lessons we could learn no other way!"

21

What Is Conviction?

About ten o'clock that evening, Dink called me from Georgia to report his findings from the trip.

"Preacha, you'll never believe it!" he declared.

I wondered if he was going to pull it on me again--- string it out, till he had exasperated me. But his excitement was too great to keep it back.

"Preacha, ders anudder body been found!!!" Then without my having to ask who, he blurted out, "Its da body of dat other robber---da guy we thought killed Sarah and da other guy."

"So, now all of those who participated in the robbery are dead? But do the authorities realize that this third guy was in on the robbery?"

"No, dey haven't tied him inta da killin of da guard, or ta da robbery, or ta his partners in crime!" he stated. "But my sources assures me dat he's one of dem!"

"Did they find the money?" I asked.

"Naw, it may be dat whoever killed all three of the da robbers has da money now!"

"Who is this guy who told you all this?" I asked.

"Dat's another mystery. He wouldn't give me his name or identity. He even seemed ta be disguised, so I'm not sure what he really looks like either. But I did get a fingerprint!" he said with some glee.

"Dink, this is getting confusing. Let me see if I can summarize what has happened so far. First, two men and a woman robbed an armored car, and killed a guard a few weeks ago. Second, one of the men and the woman were found murdered a week apart. Now the third robber is dead a few days later. The authorities know the man and the woman found first were part of the robbery, and Jasper is blamed for killing them, and they believe Jasper is the third robber. Now the real robber is dead, but the officials don't know about any part he may have had in the robbery, or even if he killed his partners. Have I got it all correct now!"

"Sure, Preacha! You'se got it now!"

"So where do we go from here?" I asked.

"Simple, " he declared. "We'se follow da fingerprint!"

"What if it leads somewhere we don't want to go!" I spoke, thinking out loud.

"Does ya want ta help Jasper, or not?" he said as he stated the obvious.

I thought to myself, "Here we go again! Round and round we go, and where it ends, nobody knows!"

As if he knew my thoughts, Dink reminded me, "Remember, we has da leadership of our sovereign providential God!!"

I thought again with some humor, "Theology can comfort, but it can also in the process get one into trouble at times!"

I told Dink to trace the fingerprint and then we could decide the next step.

Again, the next day, a Wednesday, I made a bee line to the jail when my last class was finished. Our subject for that day was conviction, and we turned in our Bibles to the clearest passage on the subject, John 16:8-11, and read it together.

8 And when he is come, he will reprove the world of sin, and of righteousness, and of judgment: 9 Of sin, because they do not believe in me; 10 Of righteousness, because I go to my Father, and ye see me no more; 11 Of judgment, because the prince of this world is judged.

In this passage Jesus is speaking of the work the Holy Spirit will perform, when He is sent by Christ into this world after His exaltation. He will do three things: reprove the world of sin, reprove the world of righteousness, and reprove the world of judgment. The Greek word for reprove here is ελεγχω, and has several shades of meaning, including, to lay bare, to expose, to rebuke, to convict, to reprove.

The Holy Spirit Will Convict of Sin
(verses 8-9)

The context seems to call for the meaning of exposing to men the reality of their sin. Admittedly, there can be an exposure of sin (a laying bare) that a man may admit, or there could be an exposure of sin (a laying bare) that a man will not admit.

Thus there is a sense in which the Holy Spirit will show the world by the gospel what sin really is, even to the extent of bringing a sense of guilt upon men for their sin, and yet they are not saved as a result. We could call this a general conviction that comes to men, yet falls short of conversion. This passage certainly speaks of this general conviction of sin upon the world.

There is another level of conviction of sin, or the bringing of a knowledge of guilt upon men, and that is the conviction which leads to salvation. This, too, comes by the preaching of the gospel. This is a special conviction of the elect. This conviction is seen in various places in the New Testament, such as on the day of Pentecost, where multitudes were smitten in their hearts and responded to the truth.

The Holy Spirit Will Convict of Righteousness
(verses 8 and 10)

The world has never possessed a true understanding of righteousness. There have been moral men who thought they understood righteousness, but their righteousness failed because they did not understand the righteousness of God. The morality of man is not true righteousness, because it is built by a sinful man for his glory on the foundation of a fallen depraved nature, which, therefore, is incapable of producing true righteousness.

Even religious men, such as the Jews of Jesus day, were not righteous, as they were the ones who crucified Him in the name of their religion and righteousness. The world is full of false religions, which claim to point to the true way of righteousness, but only the gospel of Jesus Christ possesses the message of true righteousness. Is it not strange that Jesus was rejected by the people, who called themselves God's people, but Jesus was to be received into heaven very soon of the Father, Who they claimed to be exclusively their God?

So the Holy Spirit will convince men that true righteousness is not to be found within themselves, but within God and His provision in His Son, Jesus Christ. Again, there is a general conviction in this area, as well as the special conviction, which comes to the elect and leads them to salvation.

The Holy Spirit Will Convict the World of Judgment
(verses 8 and 11)

Again, man is blind, because of his sin, to the judgment of God which rests upon the whole human race. Because man makes light of sin, and promotes his own righteousness within or without a religious context, he also does not see the reality and danger of judgment.

Thus the Holy Spirit will lay bare his false ideas in the area of the judgment of God as well. That conviction of judgment is to be tied in with the fact that the great enemy, the ruler of the world, Satan himself, has been judged already. The Greek verb here is a perfect indicative passive. The perfect indicates that the judgment sentence upon Satan was given in the past and is still resting upon him today. The indicative indicates the statement is a fact, while the passive speaks of the fact that the sentence of judgment has come from outside of himself, yea, from God.

Thus the sentence of judgment is clearly upon man, because man in his sinful nature is a follower of Satan, and not a follower of God. The Holy Spirit will lay bare this reality before men, but again the conviction of judgment will be general to some with no response, while the conviction of judgment will be special and powerful to others, leading to salvation.

The Holy Spirit speaks to men with convincement concerning their own sin, their lack of righteousness, and their coming judgment. Yet not all respond. Only those enabled by the Holy Spirit will respond to the truth.

"Wow," Jasper exclaimed. "The Holy Spirit even convicts a believer of sin when he has backslid, like He did me!! I was explodin' with conviction of sin, and my lack of righteousness, as well as because of a sense of judgment! No wonder I was so miserable, and even tried to destroy God's work by committin' more and more sin. Praise God, He wouldn't let me go!"

Then he threw in one of his southern sayings.

"My sins was enough to make a freight train take a dirt road. Praise God, He's put me back on the track."

I left the jail, went by to get Ira, and the visit was like the previous night. On the way home, I got another "sermon" from Ira, Jr.

"Daddy, trials and sorrows teach us a lot of things, don't they?"

I had no idea where he was headed, so I just nodded and agreed.

"One thing all this has taught me, is that we take a lot of things for granted, and don't really appreciate them till we are about to lose them, or even until they are gone!"

I nodded again, and gave him a strong, "Amen!"

"Now, I appreciate not only April more, but also you and mommy and Beth. We could lose each other at any time! I also appreciate my good health. I could lose it at any time. And all that God provides for us, we have a habit of taking for granted. It makes me understand also what Dink and Janie have gone through in the loss of 'little Dink.' That must have been awful to have him kidnapped, and then find out he was dead."[1]

He continued after a moment of silence.

"Daddy, I'm going home to tell mommy I love her, and then I am going to tell little Beth the same thing. And, Daddy, I love you too!"

22

Who Is the Mystery Guy?

Though I was weary, I forced myself through the next day, a Thursday. Teaching at school, teaching at the jail (and both required preparation), plus hospital and jail visits, and wrestling with the question of how we could help prove Jasper's innocence, was about to get me down. Plus this Thursday wasn't going to be much different from the previous days of this week.

It wasn't until I got a break between classes in mid-morning that I got a chance to stretch out on a couch in my office to try to sort some of these things out in my thinking.

If the third body that had just been found, could be associated with the previous two bodies as part of the robbery of the armored car, as the mystery man had told Dink, then Jasper was not one of the three robbers involved in that crime! And if it could be proven Jasper was in jail when the third man was killed, then he was not guilty of this murder. Which opened the door to ask the question, that if someone else had killed one of these three robbers, could it be that the same person had killed the other two robbers as well? That would mean that Jasper was not involved in any of these murders.

Thus we had to be sure that the authorities knew of the association of these three bodies! Which in turn made it paramount that the mystery man be found, so he could tell what he knew of all of this scenario, and link the three robbers together in the crime. But then, who killed all three of them? It could be understood that one might kill the other two, but who killed all three? What was the motive? And what had happened to the money? Could it be that someone had killed all three in order to get their hands on the money---maybe the mystery man?

Just as I was thinking that I would be very interested to learn if Dink had traced the fingerprint, he popped in! He had driven back from Georgia that morning, and had even been to the police station already.

"Hey, Preacha!" he burst forth. "Got some news on da fingerprint! But ya know, Preacha, sometin' still bothers me 'bout dat fingerprint!"

"What?" I asked, thinking he was about to share with me some important treasury of truth.

"Ya never did ask me how I'se got dat print!" he said, disappointing me.

"What's so tough about getting a fingerprint?" I asked him.

"Well, didn't I tell ya dat da guy was wearin' gloves?" he said teasing me. "How did I get a print of a guy wearin' gloves?"

Knowing I would never get the primary answer until I let Dink shine giving the secondary one first, I listened to his story of how he got the fingerprint of a man wearing gloves!

He told of arriving early at the restaurant, where they were to meet. He had been instructed to sit in a certain corner booth, and to wait for this man, who would be wearing gloves. That sounded strange to Dink, since it was not cold out at all. He figured that since the guy was wearing gloves, he was fearful of someone getting his prints.

Dink waited outside in the parking lot in the dark, and watched for a guy with gloves. Dink identified him when he got out of his car, and he approached him from behind, and knocked him out by applying force to the pressure points on the sides of the neck.[1] While he was out, he took off one of his gloves and got a good print on a small piece of glass that he was carrying. He then put the glove back on his hand, and went inside to wait at the corner table.

"Did he come in?" I asked, having gotten interested in his story? "What would you have done, if he hadn't?"

"Sure, he came in!" Dink calmly informed me. "And, really, who cares whether he came in or not. His comin' in wasn't what would've identified him ta me. It was his fingerprint! I'd rather got dat dan ta talk ta him!"

"But wasn't he suspicious, that someone had knocked him out?" I quizzed, forgetting the primary question.

"Well, he was puzzled, but not suspicious of me, cause dis method leaves ya totally disoriented with no remembrance of how it happened. And since his gloves were still on his hands, and nothin' was missin' from his pockets, he figured he had fainted. He muttered about needin' ta see a doctor soon. In God's providence unbeknownst ta my knowledge, he mighta had some medical problem already dat he blamed it on."

"So you got some spoken information out of him, as well as an identity?" I asked, wanting to get to the essentials of the matter.

"Yep!" he countered.

"Well, out with it! Who is he?" I insisted.

"He's some guy from Philadelphia wid a record da size of a freight train!" he answered.

"What's he doing here, and why is he interested in the robbery and these murders?" I asked.

"Dunno, but I'm gonna figure it out!" Dink promised.

What Is Repentance?

When I went to the jail that evening, after dropping, Ira, Jr., at the hospital, Jasper was stronger than any time since his restoration. He definitely seemed more himself.

"Ira, I sure feel better today," he assured me. "There for awhile I felt like I had reached rock bottom, but was still goin' lower!"

Then after I had filled him in on Dink's adventures, and the finding of new information that could be helpful to him, he was even more encouraged.

"You don't know how much that encourages me, Ira. I was beginning to feel not just like a has-been, but a never-will-be-nothin-ever-agin!"

Then we turned to our evening study, the doctrine of repentance. We recognized that many, for various reasons, denied the importance and the necessity of repentance. We began by noting the importance of the doctrine, giving just a few of the many verses, which stress that truth.

THE IMPORTANCE AND NECESSITY
OF REPENTANCE

1. <u>John the Baptist came forth preaching repentance</u>

In those days came John the Baptist, preaching in the wilderness of Judea, saying, Repent; for the kingdom of heaven is at hand.

Matthew 3:1

2. <u>Jesus came forth preaching repentance</u>

From that time Jesus began to preach and to say, Repent; for the kingdom of heaven is at hand.
Matthew 4:17

3. <u>The apostles held repentance foremost in their preaching</u>

Then Peter said unto them, Repent, and be baptized, every one of you, in the name of Jesus for the remission of sins, and you shall receive the gift of the Holy Spirit.
Acts 2:38

Paul says, he was: *...testifying both to the Jews and also to the Gentiles, repentance toward God and faith toward our Lord Jesus Christ.*
Acts 20:21

4. <u>God commands all men everywhere to repent</u>

But now God commands all men everywhere to repent.
Acts 17:30

5. <u>The failure to repent results in a man perishing</u>

Jesus said....*I tell you, Nay. But except you repent, you shall all likewise perish.*
Luke 13:3

Thus, who can deny the importance and necessity of repentance in light of the following summary?

if John the Baptist's emphasis was repentance
if Jesus' initial message was repentance
if Peter tied remission of sins to repentance
if Paul preached repentance both to Jews and Gentiles
if God commands all men everywhere to repent
if Jesus said without repentance a man would perish

Yet some men do deny the importance and necessity of repentance:

some claim it belongs to another age---not the NT age
some fear it will lead to salvation by works
some damage true repentance by a shallow definition
    the shedding of some tears
    the troubling of the conscience
    the determination to reform one's life
    the fear of sin's results
    the temporary reformation of one's life
    the momentary fear of God's judgment
    the confession of sin alone
    the practice of penance
    the agony of one's soul over one's sin

THE HISTORICAL DEVELOPMENT
OF THE WORDS REGARDING REPENTANCE[1]

The Words for Repentance in General

μετανοεω can mean
    to change one's mind
    to adopt another view
    to change one's feelings
    to feel remorse

μετανοια can mean
> change of mind
>> but it usually is not a function of the mind alone
>>> as it can affect feelings, will, and mind
> regret
>> remorse
>> dissatisfaction with thoughts, actions, plans
>> pain or grief over what has happened
>> can include a sense of a necessity of change needed

Thus both words carried in historical Greek the meaning
> of a change of mind which often includes
>> an emotional and volitional aspect

The Concept of Repentance
in the Old Testament[2]

There is the stress in the Old Testament
> of the seriousness of one turning from sin
> which also includes and claims the will
>> and a turning from sin to God

The Concept of Repentance
in the New Testament[3]
(John the Baptist and Jesus)

μετανοεω (the verb) and μετανοια (the noun)
> to change one's mind or a change of mind
> to convert or conversion
> these words give expression
>> to the OT concepts
>>> of religious and moral conversion

according to John the Baptist
    it is once and for all
    it must be genuine and not in appearance only
    it is demanded of all
        not just notorious sinners
        but of Jews who think they do not need it
    it is a change from within
    it is a change that must be demonstrated
        in life and actions

according to Jesus
    Jesus does not just repeat John's message
        but he surpasses it
    repentance
        is the heart of His demands of His kingdom
        is the purpose of His coming
        is the result of His display of power
        is a way that must be taken by all
        is once and for all
        includes a final decision by man
        includes an unconditional response by man
        includes a radical conversion to God
        includes a definitive turning from evil
        includes a resolute turning to God in obedience
        includes an unconditional turning to God
        includes an unconditional turning
            away from sin
            away from all that is against God
        affects the whole man
            his conduct at all times
            his thoughts
            his words
            his actions

> is more than negative---strongly positive
>> calls for total surrender of the will of man
>> calls for total commitment to the will of God

The Meaning of the New Testament Words
for Repentance

"In the N.T. the subject chiefly has reference to repentance from sin, and this change of mind involves both a turning from sin and a turning to God. The parable of the prodigal son is an outstanding illustration of this. Christ began his ministry with a call to repentance, Matt. 4:17, but the call is addressed, not as the O.T. to the nation, but to the individual. In the Gospel of John, as distinct from the Synoptic Gospels, referred to above, repentance is not mentioned, even in connection with John the Baptist's teaching; in John's Gospel and Ist Epistle the effects are stressed, e.g., in the new birth, and, generally, in the active turning from sin to God by the exercise of faith (John 3:3; 9:38; I John 1:9), as in the N.T. in general." [4]

μετανοια[5]
> repentance
> turning about
> conversion
> turning away from dead works

"Boy, anybody who'd argue with that would argue with a sign post!" Jasper declared. "To think that I used to believe that repentance was optional, and meant only a change of one's mind. I thought I was guarding the gospel, when I was actually opening the door for sin!"

We chatted for a few moments, and then I made my way to the hospital. I found Ira, Jr. in his usual place--- along side the bed of April, talking to her as if she were fully awake. Her mother was gaining strength by leaps and bounds each day, and they wheeled her down to see April for several hours a day.

After prayer we left for home, and young Ira was still talking, and maybe tonight, he was talking too much!

"Daddy, how does God's sovereignty relate to April's getting well or not getting well, and even to our praying for her to get well?" he queried.

I spoke to him as follows.

"We are on earth as God's children to glorify Him in life or in death! The time spent on earth, whether it be a few years or a hundred years, is like a drop in the ocean, compared to the ocean of eternity we will have with our Lord. We should be willing to glorify God in any manner He deems best. The Bible says that the man who gains his life loses it, and the man who loses his life, will gain it. The grain of wheat that falls into the ground and dies will bear much fruit. Thus, we bow to His sovereignty in all things regarding our own lives and the lives of our friends and loved ones. Whatever He brings into our lives, we thank Him, and submit to Him as our sovereign God, for we know His will for us shall glorify Him.

"Yet, our great sovereign God gives us the privilege, yea, He even commands us to ask and we will receive. He tells us we have not because we ask not. Those verses do not teach that He answers every prayer, for as we pray, we ask in submission to His will, as Jesus did in the garden. Remember, He prayed to His Father, 'Not my will, but Thine be done!' Many times His name is glorified as He answers our prayers, and heals our loved ones and friends.

"Thus we desire His glory, but we pray believing in submission to Him, as He commanded us, and we rejoice in His will being done, for we know it is best. Through out every trial we walk and live by faith that He is God and He knows best and that He loves us and will do the best for us. Yet we still bombard His throne with prayer in behalf of those in great need. This is what pleases Him---for us to submit to Him, to seek His face, and to trust Him in every hour and in every circumstance and result. He maketh no mistake!!"

He answered in his usual strength.

"Then faith means no matter how dark it may be, no matter how impossible it seems, no matter how sad we feel, no matter how puzzled our mind, no matter how uncertain our future, we trust our great sovereign God!"

"Amen!" I shouted.

"Amen!" he echoed, adding, "What does amen mean, Daddy?'

"It means, so be it!!!"

"SO BE IT, DADDY!!" he said, even with a few tears.

What Is Saving Faith?

I was glad the next day was Friday. Maybe I could get some rest over the weekend. I was tempted to skip my jail and hospital visits on this day, rejoicing that tomorrow was Saturday, and I could make up the missed visits then. But I knew Jasper needed the encouragement, and Ira, Jr. was eager to see April. He was waiting to go when I arrived home in the afternoon. I dropped him at the hospital, and then headed to the jail.

But as I drove, I was jarred out of my meditative and weary stupor by someone behind me honking. I could have guessed it---it was Dink. I pulled into a burger joint, and he motioned me inside. As we devoured a couple of super burgers, he filled me in on his latest caper.

"Well, what do you know?" I began. "Anything further on the mystery man or the dead folks?" I bluntly asked.

"Yep! I found out where da guy lives!" he said both informing me and boasting a little.

"Is it far from here?" I continued my mental search.

"Bout thirty miles outta da city in Georgia where Jasper pastored. He lives back in da sticks and up in da hills, where nobody could ever find him, cept me!" he crowed again flashing his humble smile.

"An dats not all!" he continued. "Two people lives wid him!"

"Could it be a man and a woman?" I asked just guessing.

"Bingo, Preacha. You gets da prize! A man and a woman!"

"But how did you find them?" I asked.

"Easy!" he assured me. "I didn't tell ya dat da other night I had an old buddy follow him home from da restaurant."

"But if its so remote, how did your buddy keep from being seen. His lights must have been visible as he followed him out in the country where there was no other traffic," I protested.

"We got ways, Preacha!" he chortled. "Electronic guidance by a transmitter on his car, and we even drive in da dark, when necessary!"

"Well, what next?" I asked.

"You an I'se goin' over der ta pay dem a visit!" he said. "We'se gonna put a sting on dem!"

I'd been through one sting with Dink, involving a harmless newspaper man.[1] But a sting with possible notorious and dangerous people---that was something else!

"What's the sting?" I asked.

"You jus' be ready bout 5:00 AM in da mornin'. I'll clue ya in den! It won't be dangerous. We're dealin' wid people who aren't too smart. It takes dem two hours ta watch sixty minutes on TV!" he sought to assure me.

As I drove on to the jail, I sighed, realizing I would not get to sleep in as I had planned. Dink had taken care of that. I thought of a Southern saying that applied to Dink. It said, "He ain't got no ulcers, but he's shonuf a carrier!"

I didn't know whether to share Dink's plans for the next day with Jasper or not. I was a little concerned that he might get his hopes up too high, or that he might tip off someone who could spoil the plans. I had found out a long time ago that it's a small world, especially in the jail system. I did ask him to keep on praying, and I told him that Dink thought we were getting closer to the truth.

Our subject for this night was saving faith. I began by pointing out that faith is one of those words like love and others of the Christian vocabulary, that we often do not take time to define. As a result these words develop a wide and general definition, which means, they become too general to be used for the Biblical meaning of faith.

I gave him some examples of how even professing Christians use faith often with a general undefined meaning. The list included the following:

"Have faith....?"
"Keep the faith, brother!"
"I have experienced the feelings of faith?"
"All you have to do is believe...."
"Never lose faith..."
"My faith carried me through!"
"I have experienced the feelings of faith!"

"Now in context," I explained, "these statements might be acceptable. But so many times they are used without a context of clear understanding or definition. Therefore, I must ask some questions!" I listed my questions as follows

Have faith! in what? in who? why?
Keep the faith, brother! in what? in who? why?
I have experienced the feelings of faith! in what? in who? how?
All you have to do is believe! believe what? believe who? why?

"I think by now you get the point!" I stated to Jasper. "The word faith is used loosely many times and never defined. It is used almost meaning have faith in faith. Never mind the definition of faith! Never mind the object of faith. Never mind the reason for faith! Never mind the content of faith!" I spoke with passion.

"Just have faith in something---anything! Have faith in faith! Have faith in yourself! Have faith in superstition! Have faith in some teacher or guru! Have faith in psychology and what it tells you! Have faith in feelings! Have faith in your experiences! Have faith in man! Have faith in the church! Have faith in tradition! Have faith in God---any god or anything, if it helps you!"

I was on a roll now!"

"Never mind the truth or falsity of the foundation! Never mind the definition! Never mind the object! Never mind the reason! Never mind the content of faith! JUST HAVE FAITH!!!"

Jasper sat nodding, enjoying that I was about to cut loose and preach!

"It is the faith, some say, that is important! Not the foundation! Not the definition! Not the object! Not the reason! Not the content! Just have faith!!!"

I quieted down a little, aware that others in the visiting room were staring.

"But is this the Biblical definition of faith?" I continued? "Not hardly, as we shall see that Biblical faith has a foundation! It has a content! It has a result!"

Then I handed Japer the following outline, and we went over it together, as I toned down my volume a little more.

I THE BIBLICAL FOUNDATION AND CONTENT OF FAITH

  A. The foundation of the faith of many today is man

    1. <u>the false foundations</u>

      a. many have faith in man

        they say
          man is good
          man is capable
          man is progressing
          man is perfectible by man

      b. many have faith in man's ideas

        they have
          faith in science so-called
          faith in psychology
          faith in philosophy
          faith in politicians
          faith in man for morals
          faith in man's opinions and ideas
          faith in man's solutions
          faith in man's ideas for the future

      c. many have faith in man's experiences

        his sensations
        his feelings
        his dreams
        his visions

his perceptions
his ideas based on experiences
his personal inspirations and revelations

even professing Christians have said
"I know what I believe. I don't care
what you, or any one else or even the
Bible says---I know what I have
experienced!"

2. the two resultant attitudes of faith in man

   a. *result number one of faith in man is*
   relativism---all things are relative

there are no absolute truths
    you believe what you want to believe
    I will believe what I want to believe
    one idea is as good as another
there are no absolutes
    except the absolute
        that all is relative
there are no absolute moral standards
    what's good for you is not good for me
    what's best for me is not best for you
one idea is as good as another
    depending on the situation
one idea may work for you and another for
    me---depending
one idea may have been better in the past
    but it is not the best for today
no one can be sure of one idea
    above another

thus we are left with an uncertainty
   uncertainty of truth of moral convictions
   uncertainty of truth concerning actions
     of right and wrong
   uncertainty of truth
     concerning good and evil
   uncertainty of truth
     concerning truth and error
but have faith anyway!!

b. *result number two of faith in man---*
tolerance for all, except for Christians

it is your faith that is important
   not the object of your faith
therefore we must tolerate all ideas
   except the idea that there are absolutes
thus there is a great dislike of Christians
   for they believe a Bible of absolutes
there is a fear we will rain
   on their parade of faith in man
thus so many speak of faith
   not in a Biblical sense
   but in a humanistic sense
     as their faith is in man

As I made these points, I looked at my watch and realized I was overtime. Jasper smiled and cracked, "Boy, I'm glad you have drunk from that fountain of knowledge, and didn't just gargle with it like my uncle!"

I smiled and replied, "I hope I'll be able just to gargle after tomorrow!"

Where Is the Money Hidden?

I didn't sleep very well that Friday evening! I had deep misgivings about tomorrow as Dink seemed to have it planned. We had been through a lot together, and he had more street smarts than any one could ever imagine. But still, it appeared to me that we were walking blindly into a lion's den. We didn't even know fully who these people were.

Nonetheless, I was waiting when Dink arrived, and he was as wide-awake as if he had never been asleep.

"Preacha, here's what we'se gonna do!" he stated as we headed for Georgia.

I was glad I didn't have to drag the plan out of him, but then again, I wasn't too sure I really wanted to hear it.

"We'se don't know for certain who dese people are."

I nodded in agreement.

"Da way I figure it, dere could be two possible scenarios here! Ya wid me, so far?" he asked.

I didn't know if he thought I was going back to sleep, or that I wasn't keeping up with his thinking.

"Yes, I'm with you!" I assured him.

"Well they might be either da gang dat robbed da armored car and shot da guard, or dey could be da people dat shot da people who robbed da armored car and shot da guard! Did ya get dat, Preacha?" he chirped.

"You say that in light of the fact that we have two sets of three people," I reasoned out loud. "Each set includes two men and a woman. One set of three is alive and the other set of three persons is dead. Either set could have robbed the bank and shot the guard. The question is, which group robbed the bank and shot the guard. The living ones probably killed the dead group, for some reason, and they also probably have the money from the robbery."

"Yeah, Preacha! We's gonna have ta call you'se Preacha Sherelock!" he kidded.

"So," I continued, "we want to find out the following things today about this living group. First, did they rob the armored car and kill the guard? Two, did they kill the other three people? Maybe they wanted to make the police think these other people pulled off the robbery, when they actually had done it. Three, do they have the money? And fourth, what was their plan of operation and motive throughout this strange and puzzling crime? Now, Dink, you answer me a question!" I insisted.

"Yeah, Preacha, ask anyting!"

"How are we going to find out all of the above? It seems like a big task to me!"

"Well, here's my plan, Preacha! We may not find out everyting today, be we'se gonna get a big snowball rollin', an' you knows how a snowball accelerates an' builds goin' down da hill!" he spoke with a certain glee.

"We'se goin' ta meet da local police when we gets inta town, before goin' out ta da hills where dey live," he explained.

Understandably, that gave me a sense of relief! We were not going it alone, but with police authority and firepower, if needed, because Dink had alerted them that this might help solve the armored car robbery case.

"We'se gonna try to get one of dem ta expose where dey got da money hidden!" he continued. "Den we'll swoop down an' catch dem red-handed! I'll fill ya in on da details as it all unfolds!" he added.

The rest of the trip of several hours was fairly quiet, as I dozed off and on while Dink drove. Soon it was light, but that didn't interfere with my snoozing and meditation on the coming events. I wondered how we were going to expose where they had hidden the money.

Finally, we pulled into the Georgia town where Jasper had pastored, and we were met by the local authorities--- two police cars and, another car, which Dink called a plain wrapper. He informed me that was trucker CB talk for a policeman or state trooper in an unmarked car. It was about 8:00 AM, and Dink and I and the plain wrapper made our way towards the house in the hills where the suspects were living. The two police cars drove out also, to station themselves in their respective places according to the plan.

When we got near the suspects' house, we separated from the plain wrapper, and we took up our place of surveillance in a thicket, and they went to another assigned spot. Dink then took the phone, which he had gotten from the police, and he dialed the number at the house to light the fire of our sting. The phone rang a few times, and when someone answered, Dink spoke.

"Let me speak to Bugsy!" he said in a gruff whispering tone, but definitely strong enough to be heard. And to my surprise, he spoke perfect English and not 'Dink' language. That was the first time since I had met him, that I could remember hearing him speak without his unique accent.

I also wondered where he had gotten the phone number, but then figured that if you have the address, the phone number is easy, especially with the police on your side.

"No, only Bugsy!" he emphasized, evidently to the question if someone else would do.

A moment of silence followed. Dink winked at me, and it was obvious that he was enjoying this to the hilt.

"Never mind who I am. And don't ask me why I am calling. I have my reasons. I have a contact who knows where the armored car robbery money is hidden. You'd better cover your tracks on that matter, before he exposes you, and all your plans to spend it will come to naught, as will any plans you have of staying out of jail for the rest of your life. And what you do, you had better do quickly! This person is super powerful, and he'll deal with you in his way when he wants!" he added.

With that he hung up! I was sure Bugsy on the other end of the line was protesting, or begging for more information, but that was it.

"Now what?" I asked Dink?

"Now we waits ta see what Bugsy does!" he explained, as he was back in 'Dink' language again.

I had to ask another question.

"Dink, who is this contact who knows where they have hidden the money?"

He looked at me and smiled.

"Da Lord!   Dat's da part of da sting!   An' dat statement's no lie. Da Lord does know where da money is! And He is a super powerful person. And He will deal wid dem as He wishes when He wants. And da Lord will in time expose dem.   We're just helpin' da Lord ta do it sooner, if dat's what He wants ta do!"

"What do we do now?" I asked.

"We just wait ta see if da sharks take da bait!" he said, as he settled back in his seat. "Keep watch on da road, an' when ya see a red Camaro comin', let me know!"

I had no idea what we would do, but nonetheless, I glued my tired eyes to the road as we hid in the thicket.

26

Where Do We Go from Here?

Ten or fifteen minutes passed, as I kept watch on the road, looking in the direction Dink had pointed. Not a single car or truck passed in that time, which was a testimony as to the remoteness of the area where we were parked. Then it happened.

"Dink, here he comes!" I said excitedly.

With that Dink was instantly awake, readied himself to start the engine, and at the same time was on his phone to the others in the sting.

"Da turkey's outta da coup headed for da slaughter!" he said, speaking into the phone.

I found out later that this meant the red Camaro was headed towards us. He would have been instructed by the plain wrapper that the turkey was out of the coup and headed for the farm, if he had gone the other direction. We let the Camaro pass, and we were so well hidden he did not see us. Then we pulled out on the road to follow at a safe distance, safe enough that the driver couldn't even see us. We, however, were tracking him also by means of the electronic guide Dink had put on his car the night they had met in the restaurant. The other police cars were moving to their next assigned places.

We had no idea whether he had the money with him and was moving it to another hiding place, or if he was going to the money, wherever it was hidden. All we could do was to follow, being careful not to expose ourselves, while we hoped we would soon see the money, whereby we could tie them to the crime. And, eventually, this would help to free Jasper from his involvement in the crimes.

As we approached the more populated area, the Camaro turned onto the interstate. Then he sped up till he was well beyond the speed limit. Soon he was going over a hundred miles an hour.

"Do you think he has spotted us?" I asked as Dink and the plain wrapper both sped up.

"He's spotted somebody!" Dink said. "Check yer seat belt!" he shouted as he floored his truck.

Soon the regular police cars were involved in the chase, with their blue lights flashing. That to a great extent cleared the way for us, but it seems some people just freeze when they see a blue light behind them. We careened down the interstate, not wanting to loose our man in the Camaro.

I had seen some of these chases on television, and I found myself very concerned, not only for us, but for some innocent people, who could be hurt by the increasing carelessness of the driver of the Camaro. I had mixed emotions about continuing this pursuit. What benefit would it bring to chase him, if in the process someone was killed in this high speed adventure?

Then it happened. The driver of the Camaro lost control of his vehicle, and plunged off the road, down an embankment, and slammed into a tree going over a hundred miles an hour. All the police vehicles, plus our truck, converged on the scene with screeching tires, and screaming sirens. By this time the Camaro was burning. As police scurried around to try to put the fire out with their small extinguishers, it was discovered that the body of the driver had been thrown clear in the crash. It was Bugsy, as

Dink identified him, and he was dead! Soon a fire truck arrived and the fire was extinguished.

When the trunk was pried open and searched, along with the other charred remains of the car, it was determined that there was no money in the Camaro! Our lead to the money, so it seemed, was gone, unless the other people in the house knew where it was. Wisely, the police had left a car to survey the house. The other two at the house could not get away, but did they know the location of the money from the robbery? And would they tell us what they knew or their part in the crime, when they were confronted with what evidence there was?

As we drove home, leaving the police to question the other suspects, we realized our desire to help Jasper for that day had ended in failure. If the money was hidden somewhere, it would be a long time till the other two of this group would go to it, even if they knew where it was. Our only hope was that the police would be able to find other evidence, or in some way be able to secure information from the man or woman who had been Bugsy's associates.

We got back into Seminary City in the late afternoon, and both of us were emotionally and physically drained. Before going home, we went to the jail to share the result of our day with Jasper. He took the news well, thanking us for our efforts, and assuring us that our labor had not been in vain (a good Bible phrase).

27

What Is Biblical Faith?

I had to admit it, after what we had been through, I wasn't eager for any further conversation, but I knew our time of study was essential for Jasper---especially the subject we were pursuing tonight. So I pulled out my notes on faith, and sought to be enthusiastic.

I reviewed, first of all, what we had seen in our previous study on faith, that is, that the church of our day has a very fuzzy, undefined concept and use of the word faith. In reality, the foundation of faith of so many today is a false one, in that it is based on a faith in man---man himself, his ideas, his experiences, his personal beliefs. The two results of the fuzzy faith we had mentioned were relativism (there are no absolute truths, only personal beliefs) and tolerance for all beliefs except for Christians, who have a strong belief in absolutes.

I also gave our outline from the previous study:

I THE BIBLICAL FOUNDATION AND CONTENT OF FAITH

   A. The foundation of the faith of many today is man

      1. the false foundations
      2. the two resultant attitudes of faith in man

I then turned to our study for this hour.

B. The Biblical foundation of faith is God

1. <u>The Biblical declaration is that God exists</u>

*For without faith it is impossible to please him;
for he that cometh to God must believe that he
is, and that he is a rewarder of them that
diligently seek him. (Hebrews 11:6)*

a. *an understanding of the teaching of this
verse*

we must have faith or we cannot please Him
we must believe that He is (exists)
we must believe that He rewards them
    that diligently seek Him
this is not just have faith in anything

b. *an understanding of the context of this verse*

it cannot be denied that the context speaks
    of the God of the Bible
    not of just any god or
    not just any concept of God

c. *an understanding of the attitude of the
Biblical writers*

divine revelation begins with God
    it never begins with the wisdom of man
divine revelation comes from God to us
    it does not start with us figuring out God

divine revelation reveals God
 men cannot find God on their own
read the first chapters of the Bible
 God is declared to exist, create, etc.
 God is not argued to exist

2. <u>God is the creator of all things</u>

Through faith we understand that the worlds were framed by the word of God, so that things which are seen were not made of things which do appear. (Hebrews 11:3)

an understanding of this verse
 God is the Creator of the world
 God created the world by His word
  He spoke and it came into existence
 God created the world out of nothing
  He did not make the things we see
  out of things already seen

3.. <u>God has certain attributes and has revealed Himself</u> (man cannot figure God out for himself)

we do not have the time to pursue all His
 attributes but they are clearly revealed to us

a. by the world He created

see Psalm 19:1
 the heavens declare the glory of God
 the firmament shows His handiwork

see Romans 1:20
>the invisible things of Him
>>from the creation of the world
>>>are clearly seen
>>>being understood
>>>>by the things which are made
>>even His eternal power and Godhead
>>>so that they are without excuse
>a summary of the Scriptural evidence
>>the created heavens declare
>>>the glory of God
>>the created earth declares
>>>His handiwork
>>the creation clearly reveals
>>>His invisible characteristics
>>>even His eternal power and Godhead
>>the creation leaves man without excuse
>>>to believe
>>>to be convinced of His existence

b.   *by His Son*

the Son is called the Word in John 1

In the beginning was the Word, and the Word was with God, and the Word was God. (vs 1)

And the Word became flesh, and dwelt among us, and we beheld His glory, the glory as of the only begotten of the Father, full of grace and truth. (vs 14)

the Son is called the Word
    because He came to reveal the Father
    in Christ we behold the glory
        of God the Father (John 1:14)
    in Christ's face shines the glory
        of God (II Corinthians 4:6)

c. *by His Word*

the written Word of God is the Bible
    it reveals God
    it reveals truth for our profitability

*All Scripture is given by inspiration of God,
and is profitable for doctrine, for reproof,
for correction, for instruction in righteousness, that the man of God may be mature,
completely prepared for all good works.
(II Timothy 3:16-17)*

THUS THE FOUNDATION OF OUR FAITH IS GOD
    as revealed to us
        in His creation---in His Son---in His Word
THUS THE CONTENT OF OUR FAITH IS GOD'S
REVELATION
    as found in His Son
    as found in His Word
    and without God's revelation as the foundation
        there is no faith---no true faith

II APPLICATION

A. Not all faith is true faith
  1. <u>true faith has the proper foundation and content</u>

  2. <u>false faith lacks the proper foundation or content</u>

     faith based on experience is a false faith
     faith based on emotion is a false faith
     faith based on feeling is a false faith
     faith based on man's ideas is a false faith
     faith based on self is a false faith
     faith based on psychology is a false faith
     faith based on philosophy is a false faith
     faith based on a guru's teaching is a false faith
     faith based on the church is a false faith
     faith based on tradition is a false faith

  3. <u>true faith has a proper attitude towards the foundation and content</u>

     false faith may say that it agrees
         with the foundation/content of true faith
     false faith
         does not have the proper attitude
             towards the foundation
             for the demons agree with the true faith
                 but tremble

  4. <u>true faith will be active and be seen by its works</u>

     just because there may appear to be works
         does not prove one has a true faith
         because a true faith must be built
             on the doctrines of the Bible

just because one says he has a true faith
does not prove one has a true faith
even though he has the beliefs of the Bible
except that claim of faith is backed up
by the presence of true Christian works
see the study in Chapter 15 of this book

B. True faith is active based on the commands and promises of God

1. <u>faith is active</u> (see Hebrews 11)

2. <u>faith is active based on the command and promise of God</u>

see Hebrews 11:7 and Genesis 6:14ff
Noah was given a command by God
to build an ark
to build it according
to God's instructions
Noah was given a promise by God
that he and his family would be saved
Noah obeyed this command and
claimed the promise by faith
thus faith is active and based
on the command and promise of God
faith without works is dead
faith is not operating in a vacuum
but operates on the basis of God's Word

III THE BIBLICAL DEFINITION OF SAVING FAITH

A. The Bible sees faith as the act of the whole man

1. <u>Saving faith includes the mind of man---it is mental</u>

   see Romans 10:17---Faith comes by hearing

2. <u>Saving faith includes the emotions of man---it is emotional</u>

   John 16---the Holy Spirit convicts man of sin,
       righteousness, judgement
   Acts 16---the conversion of the Philippian jailer

3. <u>Saving faith includes the volitional---it includes the will</u>

   not that the will can act of its own strength
   but true faith includes an act of the will
       as one is enabled by the power of God
           and casts himself on the truth of God
               which the mind has heard
               which has touched the emotions

B. Men today have seen faith as one-orbed---one of the above elements

1. <u>Some men have stressed the mental aspect only</u>

   all one has to do is agree with
       the truth content of the gospel
       or the historical facts of Jesus Christ

2. <u>Some men have stressed the emotional only</u>

they whip up an emotional atmosphere
in order to move men to decisions
without concern
for an understanding
of the truth

3. <u>Some men have stressed the volitional aspect
only</u>

they put heat and high pressure on man's will
to respond to an evangelistic appeal
without proper concern or understanding
for the truth
for the presence or absence
of the conviction of sin
the above tactics have dumped hundreds
of lost men
into the churches of today

CONCLUSIONS

1. In this day and age we must be careful to correctly and
clearly define faith

a. *true faith is not mysticism---faith in faith,
experience, etc.*

mysticism is the common ground---a general heresy
into which so many movements blend
for agreement
even though there is agreement on little else

few would argue against a person having faith
even if it is never defined with any certainty
even if there is a sell-out to man's experiences
but note such is a sell-out to extra-Biblical authority

b. *true faith is not simply agreement to a set of beliefs*

whether it be a true or a false set of beliefs
to agree with this set of beliefs
is not true faith
even though true faith is dependent on
the true set of beliefs

2. We should not be surprised at the characteristics of our
day in light of the absence of true faith

there will be a confusion of ideas
there will be a lack of discernment
there will be a lack of doctrinal clarity
there will be a lack of understanding the importance
of doctrinal clarity
there will be a relativity present
there will be a powerlessness in the church
there will be a Biblical ignorance
there will be an emphasis on feeling and experience
there will be an emphasis on religious activity
there will be a loss on the emphasis
of preaching truth and doctrine
there will be an influx of entertainment into the church
there will be an influx of supposed converts
who cannot articulate the faith
there will be a negative attitude
toward strong doctrinal convictions

there will be a lack of doctrinal purity and moral purity
there will be a loss of church discipline
there will be a dislike of doctrinal controversy
there will be a compromise
    with the world in message and ministry
there will be a lack of spiritual growth
there will be an openness
    to any and every new idea, thought and method

3. If anyone insists on using the common phrases, be sure
there is understanding of what is being said

Keep the faith, brother and sister
    this statement should have a clear understanding
        that we are not speaking of faith
            in man or man's systems
            but faith in the true God
                as revealed in the Word of God
        that we are speaking of a faith
            which is active in life
            based on commands and promises of God
        that we are not speaking of a dead orthodoxy
            faith in a set of beliefs
        that faith is the response of the whole man
            mind---emotions---will
    the same should be noted concerning
        the other common uses of the word "faith"

After reminding ourselves of God's greatness and power to answer prayer, by faith we committed all the unique events of the day to Him.

I didn't know it, but I would need that faith soon, as I headed for the hospital!

28

Why Doesn't God Answer Prayer?

I was hoping that Ira, Jr. would be in the waiting room, when I arrived at the hospital. In fact, I wouldn't even have to park, if that were the case. It was about 8:30 PM, but he was not there. So I found a parking slot, and made my way to April's room. With the day I had faced, I wasn't ready for what I encountered there.

As soon as young Ira saw me, he came over to me, grabbed me, and hugged me. I could tell he had been crying, but couldn't figure out why till he spoke.

"Daddy, April has pneumonia now! And I've been talking to the doctor and nurses. They say this is not uncommon for a person who is in a coma from having their head hit so hard. But I've also learned that many coma patients actually die from the pneumonia, and not from the injury to the head."

I hugged him for awhile, and then we prayed together, and he knew it was time to go home. He told April goodbye, kissed her on the forehead, as usual, and two worn out and weary men left the hospital that night.

The trip home was quiet for the most part. I kept wondering why a doctor or nurses, for that matter, would speak so bluntly to a little boy. But then I remembered that he was being treated as an adult by the doctor, in even allowing him to be present in the room.

Then he broke the silence.

"Daddy, God's plan is kind of hard to figure out sometimes, isn't it?"

I nodded in agreement, and let him continue.

"But when He doesn't seem to answer our prayers, that doesn't mean He has not heard us. Doesn't it just mean that He has a better plan?"

I nodded again, rejoicing that at this young age he was learning to let God be God. How many problems come in life, when we want to play God in our lives. His next remarks indicated that we were thinking on the same wave length.

"Daddy, we sure would mess up our lives, if we got everything we wanted, wouldn't we! Jesus doesn't always answer our prayers as we desire, does He? He didn't answer Mary and Martha's request to come when Lazarus was sick, did He?"

To all his questions, I kept nodding, yes!

"He had a better plan---to raise Lazarus from the dead, as an evidence that He has the power to raise all of us from the dead, someday!"

I had to be careful that all my nodding didn't turn into my drifting off to sleep.

"And, Daddy, we have to be like Jesus was even in His life. He came to do the will of His Father, even if it meant dying at thirty-three years of age. And when He was in the garden, he prayed asking the Father to remove the cup from Him. But then He prayed, 'Not my will, but Thine be done!' That's hard to pray sometimes, isn't it Daddy?"

I finally had to ask him, "Where are you getting all of this?"

"Oh, I have lots of time in the hospital to read my Bible, to think and to pray about all of these things. In fact, I've learned a lot of things I never would have learned, except by an experience like this!"

I thought to myself, "And so have I---about Ira, Jr."

29

Is Faith a Gift or Is Salvation a Gift?

I slept late the next morning, seeing it was Sunday, and rested also in the afternoon, while I planned to hit the jail and hospital in the evening. Dink called in the afternoon, to talk about the next move in the attempt to help Jasper.

"Preacha, we needs ta know who dat woman in da house in da boonies is! She probably has a record as long as Bugsy's, but it might help us ta know who she is!"

I agreed, but we couldn't figure out any way to get her identity. I suggested that maybe she would come to Bugsy's funeral, but Dink laughed and told me not to bet on it. We agreed that whoever these three people in the house were (including Bugsy), they were responsible for the death of the other three people. But how were we to get to them with no proof of their involvement in any crime? The police had combed all the crime scenes---the one where the armored car was robbed and the guard killed, and the ones also at all three sites of the murders of the three people, and even at Bugsy's death scene. Nothing! Absolutely nothing had been found that would let us get to them!

The only evidence to connect anyone to the crime was the presence of some money from the armored car robbery on the body of each of two of the three persons killed after the robbery, and the weapons of death in the first two murders, which not only belonged to Jasper, but also had his finger prints on them. The third man murdered had not been linked to the first two yet by the police, though the situation was clear to us. It was also obvious to us that these three dead people, the two men and the woman, were killed to close the police books on the case and remove any suspicion from the three in the house in the boonies. Plus, it was also clear they wanted to frame Jasper.

I dropped Ira, Jr. and Terry at the hospital, and headed for the jail. It was about 7:00 PM, and I was looking forward to adding a touch or two to the study on faith, so we could finish it. I didn't realize Jasper and I would spend most of the time talking about something else.

Immediately, when I walked into the visiting area, Jasper was ready and waiting for me. It was obvious that He couldn't contain himself, as he addressed me as soon as I was within hearing distance.

"Ira!" he shouted across the room with a deep concern and yet joy on his face. "You'll never believe what happened this afternoon! If things get any better for us, we'll have to hire someone to help us enjoy it!"

"Calm down, Jasper! What in the world could make you so delirious?" I questioned him.

"You'll never guess who visited me this afternoon!" he stated, reminding me somewhat of Dink in his ability to drag out the presentation of vital information.

"Well, you just tell me, and I won't have to guess!" I said firmly with a smile.

"Sarah Sankster!" he doted with glee.

"Sarah Sankster?" I asked in unbelief. "I thought she was dead? And who was that they buried in her place?"

"Not today! Believe me, she is very much alive. Ain't that the cat's pajamas?" he erupted again.

"What did she want?" I asked, not wondering why she would come out of hiding with a plan working so well.

"She wants me to help her!" he said.

"Help her? Help her do what?" I demanded to know.

Then he gave me the following account of her visit.

"She came in here all dolled up as fancy as I've ever seen her! She looked like a hussy! She told the jailers that she was my wife. When they told me my wife had come to visit, I got all excited, thinking it was Shirley. But then in walks Sarah! She tried to act as if everything was peachy-keen, but I was plenty cold towards her! She realized that I will probably be out of jail, eventually, just as soon as everything surfaces. It just depended on my trial coming up. She thought surely, that since the third guy had been found, I would be out of jail soon. She wants me to run off with her!"

"Run off with her? Does she think you are nuts?" I asked.

"No, she must think she is irresistible, like she was to me before. She said we could get all the money, as she would take care of the other guy at the house in the hills. We would be off scott-free, with almost five million dollars! I guess she thought that if I didn't fall for her irresistible charms, I surely would fall for her offer of the money!" he mused.

"So, what did you tell her?" I asked again.

"I tried to play it cool, and leave the door open, in case you and Dink thought there was some way we could use this to expose her to the police. Of course, no one heard the conversation between us, and it would be my word against hers that she said what she did. Ira, do you think we could use this to trap her?'

"Well, let's pray about it, and talk it over with Dink," I suggested. "He's the expert on these things!"

I could hardly wait to get home and call Dink, but now we turned to our final thoughts on faith.

We turned to Ephesians 2:8-9, and I read:
8 For by grace are you saved through faith; and that not of yourselves; (it is) the gift of God: 9 Not of works, lest any man should boast.

"The real question here is, what is it that is the gift of God? Faith or the total work of salvation? The Greek is not absolutely clear here. It could be either of the following:

Possibility One
> Salvation is by the grace of God through faith.
> Salvation is not of ourselves.
> <u>Salvation</u> is the gift of God.
> Salvation is not by works.
> If salvation were by works, men would boast.

Possibility Two
> Salvation is by the grace of God through faith.
> Salvation is not of ourselves.
> <u>Faith</u> is the gift of God
> Thus salvation is not by works
> If salvation were by works, men would boast.

"It is true that salvation is spoken of as the gift of God in other places in Scripture (see Romans 5:15-18, 6:23, etc.) But either way, whether one takes the salvation to be the gift of God in the Ephesians 2:8 passage, or that faith is the gift of God, you still come out at the same place with faith being the gift of God.

"Let me put it this way If the text is saying that <u>faith is the gift of God</u>, then it is not the work of man, but it is the work of God within man enabling man to have the faith.

Thus man is not the author nor the power of faith. Man is not passive in the matter of faith, but man is not the power nor source of faith. But the power and source of faith is God. It is a gift and not the work of man.

"If the text is saying that <u>salvation is the gift of God,</u> then every part of salvation is part of the gift, which means the following are part of the gift: conviction, calling, regeneration, repentance, saving faith, justification, sanctification, adoption, perseverance, etc. This, obviously, makes faith the gift of God. Then it is not the work of man either, but it is the work of God within man, which enables man to have the faith. Thus man is not the author nor the power of faith. Man is not passive in the matter of faith, but man is not the power nor source of faith. Rather the power and source of faith is God. It is a gift and not the work of man.

"The point is that either way one takes Ephesians 2:8-9, that is, whether it is the faith or the salvation which is the gift of God, one come out at the same place! Man is not the source nor the power of faith. God is the source and power of faith. Man believes in the gospel only as God enables. If it were any other way, man could boast in himself because of the presence of salvation in his life."

"Whoa, that pretty well settles it, don't it!" Jasper spoke in amazement. "That's gooder than grits!" he exclaimed again. "If salvation is the gift of God based on the grace of God, then how can a man lose that salvation?"

After prayer, it was off to the hospital again. The news wasn't any better concerning April, but it was very good concerning Shirley. Soon she would be released from the hospital, and could visit Jasper in jail. I had mixed emotions about sharing the news of Sarah Sankster's visit to see Jasper, but I decided she needed to know. Thus I assured her that she meant nothing to Jasper, but Sarah might lead us to the money and the proof needed to nail her and release Jasper.

On the way home, I wasn't sure Ira, Jr. would open up as before, in light of his mother being present in the car, and not a party to our little sessions of theology. But this didn't seem to matter to him.

"Daddy, a lot of good things come out of pain, and trials, and suffering, don't they?" he asked.

I hadn't informed Terry that I don't answer him during these times, but just let him go on in his theologizing. She seemed satisfied to sit back and listen also.

"I noticed today in the Bible that the apostle Paul suffered a lot too, but yet many good things came out of his suffering. Didn't he write several of his Bible books, while he was in prison? Prison is never comfortable, but I would guess that in Paul's day prisons were horrible---cold in the winter, hot in the summer, food that was sickening (if you even got that), a board or rock for a bed, and inmates that Paul would probably call 'lewd fellows of the baser sort.'"

I could tell he had been reading Acts 17:5!

"So what we need to do in all these difficult times of life, is to trust the Lord," he continued. "Isn't that right, Daddy? Then we will learn His better plan, maybe not right away, but someday. Thus we have to walk by faith and trust Him, and Him alone."

I nodded again, and winked at his mother in the front seat beside me. She smiled, and I could tell she was enjoying this also.

"There's only one thing wrong with that, isn't there Daddy? Submitting to the Lord and waiting on Him in such a difficult and impossible moment is easier to talk about and even agree with in principle, than it is to do it!"

Is God's Discipline Worth the Pain?

The next day was Monday, and being exhausted, I coasted through the day, doing only what was absolutely necessary. I had called Dink the night before to fill him in on the Sarah Sankster situation. He was shocked, as I had been, and said he would look into it right away. Then, as I was about to leave my office at school, the Dink man stumbled in.

"Well, dis ting has taken another twist dat ya won't believe!" he began, with that smirking smile on his face, which told me he knew something I didn't, and that he might string it out for awhile!

"Dink, level with me immediately!" I insisted. "It's been a long weekend, and a long several weeks. I'm exhausted, and not interested in playing any word games!"

My statement didn't seem to rattle him, but he did get to the details immediately.

"Da gal claimin' to be Sarah Sankster walked inta da local police station over der in Georgia, and gave herself up! She's da lady in da country house, and it ain't Sarah Sankster! Its her identical twin sister!!" he revealed. "Well, you'll never guess what her story is now!" he stated, slipping back into his old habit.

"Dink, get on with it!" I said again, looking askance at him.

"Oh, sorry, Preacha!" he apologized. "She claims da followin' tings now: 1) Dat da other three people (da dead ones---includin' her sister) are da ones who pulled da robbery an' killed da guard. 2) Dat Jasper den rubbed out two of dem, and one of his buddies killed the third one. 3) Dat her group of three was brought in by da other three to give da other three an alibi at da time of da crime---twin sisters look alike, etc. 4) Dat her group of three people just took da money, and split it in thirds, wid each one getting a third share. You followin' all of dis, Preacha?" he asked.

I nodded, and he picked up the story again.

"Dis is da most unbelievable part! She brought her share of da money inta da police station, and surrendered it to da authorities! She said she wanted ta make a clean break wid da crime, 'cause it had gone too far, and she was too open for false accusations for committin' some of dose crimes. She said she would be glad ta spend time in jail fer havin' da stolen money fer several weeks, an anyting else, but she didn't want to be arrested and accused of da robbery or any of da murders or even as an accomplice of any of dose crimes!"

"What about the third man in the house with her and Bugsy?" I asked.

"She said he's done split, takin' his money wid him, and she don't know where he's at!" he explained.

"And what does she say has happened to Bugsy's one-third cut in the robbery?" I asked again.

"She don't know where he hid his cut, and she has no clue as to how to find it---so she claims!" he said with a smile.

'Yeah, so she claims!" I echoed. "Nothing like a good story to save your own skin from involvement in some crimes. So she does a few years time for having the crime money for a few weeks, and other minor matters! Then she gets out of jail, and she and the third guy have two-thirds of five million dollars, if she can trust him. Or even if he's gone off on his own, she has about a third of the money. Plus she has saved herself from the death penalty. If she does nothing more than save herself from execution, she's accomplished something!"

"Youse got it, Preacha!" he agreed.

"Now, how do we prove her wrong?" I asked.

"Dats da million dollar question right now, even da life an death question fer Jasper, cause her story might be da end of any hope fer him!" he reflected.

On the way home, I went by the jail and shared all of this with Jasper. He was crushed, angry, and expressed a little bitterness.

"How can a woman lie like that, and people believe her?" he complained. "I just don't understand it---that is, how gullible people can be!"

"They'll believe her the same way you believed her sister when she lied to you---which is what got you into this mess to begin with!" I challenged, bringing him back to reality.

While there, I reviewed with him what we had studied concerning salvation thus far.

CONVICTION

This is the work of the Holy Spirit to convince a man of his sin. Because of the fall, man is blind in his mind, and not able to understand the truth about God or himself. Until God convicts him, he lives under the delusion that he has no spiritual need, that he is spiritually capable and that he is able to save himself. He is so blind that he believes salvation can be obtained by his own works. He will live in this blinded state till the Holy Spirit convicts him, showing him the truth concerning sin, righteousness and judgment. Obviously, he cannot convict himself, any more than he can save himself. He is totally dependent upon God to open his heart to the truth about spiritual matters, even concerning the depth of his sin and depravity before God.

REGENERATION

Regeneration is the work of the Holy Spirit whereby the elect are given a new principle of spiritual life. Regeneration is dependent upon God also, as the very need for regeneration indicates that a man is dead in sin, and cannot give himself life in the spiritual realm, anymore than a man who is physically dead can give himself physical life. Thus regeneration is dependent upon the Biblical doctrine of election, which says that God has chosen a people from the foundation of the world based upon His will and not upon anything in man. Regeneration does not come because of anything a man does, but it is the sovereign work of God based on His will from eternity past, whereby He has chosen a people for Himself.

REPENTANCE

Repentance is the work of the Holy Spirit whereby the elect, having been regenerated, have also a change of mind, heart and will concerning sin. Repentance again is the work of God in a man, but it is not that man is passive in the work. Man is enabled by the Holy Spirit as the result of conviction and regeneration to change his attitude towards sin, having been convicted, and to change his will concerning sin, as he now desires and turns to God for all his spiritual need.

SAVING FAITH

Saving Faith is the gift of God whereby a man, enabled by the Holy Spirit, casts himself on the word of God concerning the person and work of Jesus Christ, and concerning the promise of the Word for salvation from sin. It is the work of God for his elect, as are the other areas discussed above. Man in his natural state is not capable of saving faith. It is the work of God. True faith will be followed by true Christian works.

JUSTIFICATION

Justification is the work of God whereby the sinner through grace alone through saving faith alone is declared by God to be righteous before Him by a legal decree. Through Christ all the demands of God's law against us have been satisfied, and He then becomes our righteousness, as we have none of our own. Justification is not experiential nor subjective, but rather it is objective and outside our experience. It is the declaration of God that we are seen by Him and received by Him as righteous, because of the righteousness of Christ, because of His person and work for us, even though we in reality are sinners.

"I trust it is becoming clear," I added, "that salvation is of the Lord from start to finish! Jesus is the author and finisher of our faith!"

Jasper chimed in to agree, "It's a good thing it is, or none of us could or would be saved! That's something I've changed my mind about. I saw man too strong and too active in his ability to save himself, or contribute to his salvation. I believed Jesus was the Savior, but I gave man too much strength and power in the work of salvation. I thought man controlled and dictated to God as to when he would get saved, and even how long he would be saved. I never saw the great depth of salvation---that it was of God from the beginning to the end! Only on the basis that salvation is completely of the Lord can anyone have any confidence that it will last forever.

"Salvation is a much deeper work than I thought. If a man can save himself, or contribute to his salvation, or dictate when he could be saved, he could also call the shots concerning the loss of his salvation."

He smiled, showing the old Jasper pizzazz, as he gave a clap of his hands, along with the old mantra, "I'm saved, sanctified, livin' above sin, and striven to get in. How in the world did I ever believe that?" he exclaimed.

After laughing, and then praying, I left for the hospital, where Terry had dropped off Ira, Jr. Ringing in my mind was the Bible truth that the Lord chastens them that He loves. He disciplines us, when we are undisciplined, to teach us discipline in the living of the Christian life. Surely the results of our sin as His children are part of His discipline.

As I thought of Jasper and the discipline he faced because of his sin, I saw God's hand clearly. He puts us in a position of helplessness because of our sin, so we will learn there is no help but Him. He allows us to sense the sorrow, regret, and disappointment of sin, so we will loathe sin and not go that way again. He even allows us to think the road ahead is hopeless, so that we will cry out to Him, and learn dependence for every step.

How much better never to go the way of sin as a believer, yet how blessed to know His discipline is pure though painful!

31

What Will It Be---Earth or Eternity?

I had not intended to spend a long time at the hospital, since it was well past suppertime by now, and Ira, Jr. had already been there for an extended period of time. But when I arrived, April had taken a turn for the worse. She was in critical condition, not expected to live through the night, as the pneumonia was not reacting to medication. Her mother and young Ira were in her room, when I arrived.

I was torn between staying there or going back to the jail to share the sad news with Jasper. I decided to call Dink, and let him go to the jail, while I stayed with Ira, April, and her mother. Terry came also, but there was nothing any of us could do but wait. And waiting is the most difficult thing to do, regardless of the circumstances.

We prayed and cried, off and on, and young Ira and her mother hovered over April constantly, still talking to her through their tear-drenched eyes.

"April Showers!" Ira would state, "You're the best friend I've got! From the first time we met, I could always talk to you! I even liked your Georgia accent!" he would say kiddingly. "No one could ever say prayer like you did ---praaaaay-yeer! Or Jesus---Jaaaaay-sus! You would always ask me, 'Ira, do yah love Jaaaaay-sus?' And if I ever laughed, it wasn't at the question, but because I loved your accent!"

Then he would sit fighting back the tears until he composed himself. Then he would begin again.

"April Showers! Do you remember the first time we met? We were both new at school, and the other kids were in their groups. So you looked at me and said, 'I ustah live in Savannah, Jawjah. Where yew come from, Mistah Ira Poiyunter? An do yah know and love Jaaaaay-sus?' I never told you, but from then on you were my favorite friend."

Sometimes he would get very serious.

"Miss April Showers! You can't leave me now. We've got too many dreams to dream, and secrets to share, and lives to give for Jesus. I've still got so much to say to you! You're the prettiest girl I know, cause you're not only pretty on the outside, but you're pretty on the inside too!"

Then he would pray for her. It was always a submissive prayer, but it was very touching as a little boy went to his Father's throne to intercede fervently for his favorite little friend! I found myself crying, and wondering how the Father could ever deny such a humble, heart-broken request.

As we waited, the hours seemed like days. Ira kept up his steady talking and praying. Her mother stood by holding her hand. I was there to encourage them all in any way I could. The nurses and doctors continued to work with her. And April continued to breath---one moment at a time, as it seemed each breath might be her last one.

Then we all got a surprise! In walked Dink and a police officer with Jasper! I didn't ask how he got permission to come, but I supposed Dink had pulled some strings. It was again a very heart-wrenching scene, as Jasper and Shirley embraced, and Jasper apologized all over again, with a spirit of true repentance and sorrow. Then they sat by the bed, holding hands, crying intermittently, praying constantly, and waiting on the will of their heavenly Father.

I couldn't help in this hour but to think of a poem I had once learned about sin and its deceitful and destructive power:

Vice is a monster of such frightful mein,
That to be hated needs but to be seen;
But seen too oft, familiar with its face,
We first endure, then pity, then embrace.

I might have added that we then sorrow and grieve, not only over sins' failed promises to bring the rewards and joy we expected and wanted for ourselves, but also of its negative and unwanted results, not only to ourselves, but to other innocent bystanders around us---to say nothing of our helplessness in the face of those results. It is then that we learn what kind of fools we are, to think we can play the game of sin with the great enemy, the devil, and come away a winner. The odds would be better of breaking the bank in Las Vegas every night of one's life, than to play the roulette game of sin with Satan and win. Pity the poor fool who thinks he can play with sin, and gamble with the devil, and come away a winner!

As the night wore on, the tension built with every report from a nurse or doctor who looked in on April. We heard each time the words, "She's holding her own!" I wondered how long it would be until the final answer came, as the Lord was holding her between earth and eternity.

32

What Is Sanctification?

Since none of us had eaten anything since lunch, we began heading to the hospital cafeteria for short breaks to eat. Finally, at about 3:00 AM. Jasper and I went down for some coffee and a sandwich. I never would have suggested it, but Jasper asked if we could look quickly at the Word of God for the few moments we were eating. I concluded that since I had my notebook in the car for our studies, that we might as well cover some of that doctrinal ground concerning salvation. Our subject of thought was sanctification. I turned my notebook sideways, so he could follow as I spoke.

INTRODUCTION

The place of sanctification in the work of salvation:

1. Regeneration changes us at the core of our being. Justification changes our judicial standing before God. Sanctification changes us in our actions and life.

2. By regeneration we are changed within and by sanctification we are changed without in our actions to reflect the reality of our regeneration.

3. By justification we are declared righteous at the throne of God by faith in the work of Christ for sinners and by

sanctification we are made to be righteous by the work of the Holy Spirit within us.

4. By justification God does a work for us at the throne of God, and by sanctification God does a work in us.

5. Justification has to do with our acceptance by God, while sanctification speaks of the result of that acceptance by God in our practical daily life.

6. Errors made concerning justification and sanctification:

   a. The confusing of the two, so that one would see his acceptance before God to be based on the work of sanctification instead of justification.

   b. The separation of the two, so that one thinks he can be justified (accepted of God), and never evidence the work of sanctification in his life.

I   THE TWO SIDES OF SANCTIFICATION

   A. The work of God whereby in the work of salvation He sets us apart <u>from sin</u>

   B. The work of God whereby we are set apart <u>to God</u> for the living of a holy life.

II THE THREE TIME ELMENTS IN SANCTIFI-CATION---PAST, PRESENT AND FUTURE

A. <u>Initial Sanctification</u> is the aspect of sanctification spoken of above whereby we are at the moment of salvation set apart to God for holiness of life.

By the which will we are sanctified through the offering of the body of Jesus Christ once for all.
Hebrews 10:10

For by one offering he hath perfected forever them that are sanctified.
Hebrews 10:14

thus every believer is a sanctified person
    set apart from sin to God
    for holiness of life
thus believers are called saints
    God has set us apart to Himself

B. <u>Progressive sanctification</u> is a continuing process in the believer's life whereby the Holy Spirit conforms us more and more and little by little into a greater image and likeness of Christ.

thus the believer is told
    that he is transformed (being transformed) into
        the same image from glory to glory as from
        the Lord the Spirit---see II Corinthians 3:18
    that he is to grow in the grace and knowledge of
        Christ---see II Peter 3:18
    that he is to increase and abound in his life---
        see I Thessalonians 3:12
    that there is a perfecting of holiness---see II
        Corinthians 7:1

that God has given to the church pastors and teachers for the perfecting of the saints in the likeness of Christ, till at last they attain unto the fullness of God's standard, even Jesus Christ---see Ephesians 4:11-15

C. <u>Final sanctification</u> is the culmination of the work of progressive sanctification, which takes place at the second coming of Christ, whereby we are wholly or fully sanctified, that is, conformed completely to the image of Christ.

thus the believer is told further

that God's end is to establish his heart unblameable in holiness before Him at the coming of Christ with all His saints---see I Thessalonians 3:13

that when he sees Christ he will be like Him---see I John 3:2

that Paul pressed on to this hour with great diligence and commitment---see Philippians 3:12-14

CONCLUSION

God has been and is and will continue to work in the believer to bring him to the fullness of Christ in his life and experience. God is doing the work through the ministry of the Holy Spirit based on the work of the Son for the elect. As the believer walks in submission to Christ His Lord, the Spirit of God works the will of God for us as He works the will of God within us. And be assured that sanctification will be present in every believer in some measure or another, as we are told to follow after holiness, without which, no man shall see the Lord (Hebrews 12:14).

Time had passed quickly during our sandwich and spiritual meal. I agreed with Jasper when he noted that the progress of sanctification can be thwarted and interrupted by man's sin and rebellion. I added again that this is true! But such action is not without the loving discipline and chastisement of our gracious Father, I reminded him, as He uses even such rebellion to teach us many lessons and to bring greater progress in the work of sanctification.

"I know that even though these days have been more painful than one could imagine," Jasper admitted, "I will never be the same! I have grown more through the few months of this horrible experience, than I did most of the rest of my life put together."

When we had closed our time of study with prayer, we raised our heads, and young Ira stood before us with a big gapping smile from ear to ear!

"Daddy, the doctor says that April is going to make it! He doesn't understand it, but she has begun to respond to the medicine for her pneumonia, and sometime during the night she stabilized. We know the Lord did it, don't we, Daddy!"

We had a short prayer of thanksgiving, and then rushed back up to her room, where there was a spirit of joy and celebration and praise. It was well after 4:00 AM by now, and after further prayer and thanksgiving, we scattered, leaving April in the hands of the Lord and the hospital staff.

There was no theologizing on the way home---even young Ira was too tired. But he did say, "Now, we have to pray April out of that coma, don't we Daddy!"

With that, I heartily agreed!

33

What Is the Perseverance of the Saints?

I was glad that my classes on Tuesday were a little later in the morning, and in the early afternoon. That allowed me to sleep a few hours, and then meet both classes on time, though I was dragging somewhat. I had a late afternoon appointment with Dink (surprise---he seldom made appointments, but just dropped in).

As I looked over my notes for my visit with Jasper later in the day, Dink appeared, with his usual joviality.

"Hey, Preacha! We'se hittin' on all cylinders now!" he said, and then paused, as usual, for my reaction.

"Well, just get one more cylinder working for me---the one that keeps your mouth going till the whole story is out!" I chided him again.

"Oh, sorry, Preacha!" he said with a smile. "I keep forgettin' dat you'se is an up-front man when I'm tellin' a story! Well, ta get right to it, dat its been confirmed dat da real Sarah Sankster is dead!! She was da one killed and buried!"

Then, Dink just couldn't resist his old pattern, as he paused to get my reaction.

"Okay, Dink!" I volunteered. "You want a question before you continue? Well, here it is. Has it been confirmed that the woman who appeared to Jasper in jail is Sarah Sankster's identical twin sister?"

"Absolutely and positively confirmed!" he stated.

"And how is it that you are so positive?" I asked again.

"I'se got connections!" he assured me. "I contacted an old gangster historian (ya didn't know we had sucha ting in da Almondine, did ya), and I asked him about twin sisters who had worked wid or in da organization. He came up wid several, an' da rest was justta do a little police work gettin' pictures, etc., an' bingo, der dey were!"

"So the lady we are dealing with now is Sarah Sankster's twin sister. They are identical in looks to be able to fool Jasper!" I noted. "What do we do now to expose her and to get Jasper out of the middle of this mess?"

"I'm still tinkin 'bout dat. We could go several ways, but let me tink on it tonight. She ain't goin' nowhere, unless somebody spooks her!"

"One more question, Dink. Why is she not in jail now, after her confession?" I asked.

"She's out on bail. I don't know where she got da money. It's not da robbery money. All dey got on her so far is havin' some of da robbery money."

After some rest, and a light bit of supper at home, I made my evening rounds---young Ira to the hospital, and then on to the jail to see Jasper. I shared Dink's findings (he was still arguing that it was Sarah Sankster), and he was shocked. He would have staked his life on the conviction that the woman who visited him was Sarah Sankster!

Our subject for this hour was the perseverance of the saints. I began by explaining that this area of truth had two sides---the positive side and the negative side.

The doctrine of perseverance follows not only Biblically, but also logically from all we have seen thus far. It flows from the following premises. Thus our discussion here can be brief, as we recall what we have already studied as the basis for this doctrine:

> If God has chosen us before the foundation of the world
> If God the Father gave the elect to the Son
> If God has effectually called us into His grace
> If God has regenerated us
> If God has given us a mystical union with Christ
> If God has given us the gifts of repentance and faith
> If God has sealed us with the Holy Spirit
> If God has justified us on the basis of Christ's work
> If God has adopted us into His family as a son
> Then we can never be removed from that state
>> completely, whereby we lose our salvation and do not attain eternity with Christ, even though a true believer can be overcome with evil and fall into sin
> Thus the work of divine grace, begun by the Holy Spirit
>> in the elect's heart, will continue and be brought to its appointed end of salvation

I pointed him once again to the following verses, though we had considered some of them in detail previously (see Chapter 10):

John 10:27-29

> *27 My sheep hear my voice, and I know them, and they follow me. 28 And I give unto them eternal life; and they shall never perish, neither shall any man pluck them out of my hand. 29 My Father who gave them to me, is greater than all, and no man is able to pluck them out of my Father's hand.*

Philippians 1:6

> *Being confident of this very thing, that he who has begun a good work in you will perform it unto the day of Jesus Christ.*

Romans 8:35-39

> *35 What shall separate us from the love of Christ? Shall tribulation, distress, or persecution, or famine, or nakedness, or peril, or sword? 36 As it is written, For thy sake we are killed all the day long; we are accounted as sheep for the slaughter. 37 Nay, in all these things we are more than conquerors through him that loved us. 38 For I am persuaded that neither death, nor life, nor angels, nor principalities, nor powers, nor things present, nor things to come, 39 Nor height, nor depth, nor any other creation, shall be able to separate us from the love of God, which is in Christ Jesus our Lord.*

I also added some other verses:

II Timothy 1:12

> *For I know Whom I have believed, and am persuaded that He is able keep that which I have committed unto Him against that day.*

II Thessalonians 3:3

> *But the Lord is faithful, Who will establish you, and keep you from the evil one.*

Romans 11:29

For the gifts and calling of God are without repentance.

Thus the coin of perseverance has two sides. Side one is positive and says we will make it through to the fullness of salvation in eternity because our salvation is the work of God from start to finish---salvation is of the Lord! Side two is stated in the negative and says we cannot lose our salvation for the same reason, that it is His work in us and not a salvation by our works or by a mixture of faith plus our works. This does not deny man's responsibility in the work of salvation, but man's responsibility must be seen as unfolding under the umbrella of God's work in us in accordance with His will from eternity past.

To state it in any other manner puts God's part under the umbrella of man's will and purpose, giving man the power to negate, nullify, dictate, invalidate, thwart, impede, frustrate, foil, stymie, hinder, obstruct, block, or short-circuit the will and purpose of God.

"Wow! That's pretty strong, Ira! Not to argue, but to get some more light, what about the verses which are used so often against the perseverance of the saints? Like Hebrews 6:4-6? And others? Can we look at some of those?"

I readily agreed that we would consider in our next study the verses and arguments of those who believe salvation can be lost.

After a short time at the hospital, we were headed home a little earlier than usual. April continued to improve, but she was still in a coma!

34

What about Hebrews 6:4-6?

As I went to bed this Tuesday evening, I found myself wondering how much longer I could keep such a schedule going. I noticed that young Ira was also extra tired, in light of the all-nighter we had pulled Monday evening. I did feel somewhat refreshed Wednesday morning as I crawled out of bed, and rushed off to school.

I hadn't seen or heard from Dink, and hoped I might be blessed with one of his unexpected visits, even during this busy day. When I hadn't heard anything from him, and couldn't reach anyone at his house by 4:00 PM, I made my way home, had supper, and was off for the evening rounds.

The first thing I asked Jasper was if he had heard from Dink, and when his answer was negative, I plunged into our study of the verses some used to argue the loss of salvation. I had decided to begin with Hebrews 6:4-6, which seemed to be the favorite of those who deny the perseverance of the saints.

HEBREWS 6:4-6

4 For it is impossible for those who were once enlightened, and have tasted of the heavenly gift, and were made partakers of the Holy Spirit, 5 And have tasted the good word of God, and the powers of the world to come, 6 If they shall fall away, to renew them again unto repentance, seeing they crucify to themselves the Son of God, and put him to an open shame.

I WHO WERE THE RECIPIENTS OF HEBREWS?

the recipients were second generation Jewish Christians
    who had professed faith in Christ
    who had manifested Christian works and love
    who had served the other saints
    who had formerly endured great suffering
    who were known by the author
    who had been in contact with the author

See the following passages to establish the above:
    1:1   2:3   3:1   6:9-10
    10:32-34   13:19   13:23

II WHAT WERE THE RECIPEINTS DOING AND NOT DOING?

The total picture seems to be as follows:
    this is a group of Jewish believers
    who had professed faith in Christ
    but are now thinking of leaving Christ
        and His full work for their salvation
    because of their love for the OT and its ritual
        which love has been enhanced
        by what they are suffering as Christians

See the following passages to establish the above:
    1:4-12   2:1-3   2:18   5:11   10:35
    12:3-4   12:5ff   Chapters 7-10

III WHAT WERE THEY IN DANGER OF DOING?

They were in danger
> of letting the truth slip away
> of hardening their hearts against the truth
> of defecting from God
> of not entering into full rest in Christ
> of missing the full truth of the Word of God
> of turning loose of their profession of faith
> of going back to the Old Covenant and Judaism

See the following passages to establish the above:

2:1	3:7-8	3:12	3:13	3:15
4:1	4:2-3	4:14	10:2	12:15

IV WHAT DID THEY NEED TO DO?

They needed
> to relearn the basic elements of faith in Jesus Christ
>> to advance beyond initial Christian doctrine
>> to go on in faith, patience and perseverance
>> to grip the truth with strong persuasion
>> to lay hold of the hope set before them
>> to hold fast their profession---no wavering
>> to learn the fruit of true faith
>> to look to Jesus Christ supremely and attentively

see the following passages to establish the above:

5:12	6:1-2	6:18	10:24	10:26
10:36	11:1ff	12:1	12:2	

Final Summary
> These are Jews who have professed faith in Christ,
> but who are now considering a return to the old

Jewish faith and covenant. The question is, what is their condition now (are they really saved), and what will be their spiritual condition if they were to go back to Judaism?

V WHAT IS THE MESSAGE OF THE AUTHOR OF HEBREWS FOR THESE PROFESSING JEWS?

To convince them of continuing in their profession of faith, the writer of Hebrews argues the superiority of Christianity.

A. Jesus Christ in His person is greater than the angels
B. Jesus Christ in His position is greater than Moses
C. Jesus Christ in His priesthood is greater than Aaron
D. Jesus Christ in His performance and provision in His New Covenant work is greater than the provision of the Old Covenant

Summary

Thus the context of the book of Hebrews is that the author is addressing Jews who have professed faith in Christ, who are now considering a return to Judaism. He is seeking to convince them of the superiority of the New Covenant over the Old Covenant, and of the necessity of continuing in the former rather than to return to the latter.

VI WHAT IS THE MESSAGE OF THE WRITER IN CHAPTER 6 FOR THESE PROFESSING JEWS WHO ARE CONSIDERING A RETURN TO JUDAISM?

A. Question: Are these saved people?

1. <u>The author of Hebrews addresses them as believers</u>:

   he calls them holy brethren   3:1
      who are partakers of a heavenly calling
   he includes them in those who have believed 4:3
   he says they have a great high priest   4:14
   he says they are only spiritual babes   5:11-14
      who are not capable of strong meat

2. <u>The author also recognizes another possibility</u>

   he calls to their attention in 3:6 the possibility
      that these may not be truly saved people

   a. he tells them they are Christ's house IF they
      hold fast the confidence and rejoicing
      of the hope firm unto the end

   b. he is not telling them that by doing this
      they are made Christians or kept saved
      but he sees this as the proof of their
      salvation---perseverance to the end

   c. he calls to their attention those among the
      people of God in the OT times who
      were not truly the people of God as
      their hearts were filled with unbelief
      and therefore they did not enter into
      the rest of God

d. he states in 4:3 that we who have believed
    do enter into rest---a statement that
    recognizes again some who did not
    believe and did not enter into rest

e. he is saying that it is not a matter of one
    continuing so that he may not lose
    his salvation, but it is a matter of
    proving the reality of their salvation

f. he warns that if they have received the
    marvelous enlightening grace in such
    an amazing manner as described in
    verses 4-6, and yet have not been truly
    saved, that now if they fall away and
    go back to Judaism, it will be impossible
    to bring them back to the point of repen-
    tance once again

g. he gives a reason for this impossibility---
    they crucify to themselves the Son of
    God afresh, and put Him to open shame

h. he tells them in 6:7-8 that the proof of sal-
    vation is fruit, and the proof of being
    lost is lack of fruit

i. he tells them further after this bold pointed
    challenge that he is persuaded of better
    things for them (6:9), that he is aware of
    the evidence of their salvation (6:10),
    but that he is desirous of their giving full
    evidence of their salvation (6:11-12)

3. <u>The context thus guides us in interpreting 6:4-6</u>

   a. these phrases do not speak of salvation

      those who were once enlightened
      those who have tasted the heavenly gift
      those who were made partakers of the Spirit
      those who have tasted the good word of God
      those who have tasted the future world

   b. these phrases speak of people

      who have been with God's people
      who have been blessed by such association
      who have been spiritually enlightened
      who have tasted of the blessing of salvation
      who have partaken of the reality of the Spirit
      who have tasted the good word by preaching
      but they have not been saved!

   c. this is the challenge the writer gives to them

      Continue in the faith and it proves salvation
      Return to Judaism and prove you are lost
      But even worse than proving one is lost
         one is left in an unsavable state
         as a return to Judaism
            closes the door to being brought
               to the plateau of salvation again
               to the possibility of repentance
               to the previous enlightenment

> leaves them in a lost estate forever
> as they are rejecting Christ
> putting Him to open shame
> agreeing with His crucifixion
> what a horrible state that will be

d. but remember above that the author says

> he is persuaded of better things for them
> he is persuaded they possess true salvation
> their actions will not keep them saved
>> but prove if they were ever truly saved

I then added, as I had noted to him previously, that if this passage teaches one can lose his salvation, then it proves more than the Arminian wants to prove. It teaches that the one who loses his salvation, cannot ever be saved again. Thus it is not once saved, always saved, but it is once saved, never to be saved again if salvation is ever lost.

After discussion and prayer, Jasper's heart was full. He realized that only the grace of God that saved him, had been the power that kept him, even in the midst of his straying from the Lord. As we rose from prayer, we came face to face with old Dink's smiling face. He had unknown information written all over his smiling countenance, also.

"Hey, you'se guys will never believe what I learned taday! What price ya willin' ta pay me fer it?" he said jokingly.

When he saw our scowls and disturbed faces, he backed up.

"Just kidden!" he said hastily. "I will give you a hint, though, if ya wants one!"

35

What Is This Story Dink Is Telling?

After toying with us for awhile, Dink finally spit it out. I figured it must be something quite important, in light of the big deal he made out of it.

"I found da money!!!" he finally said with exuberance. "I turned it over ta da police already!"

"All of it?" I asked, tempering my excitement till I was sure he was on the level and not joshing us.

"All of it---'cept what Sarah Sankster, Jr. (his name for the twin sister) brought in a few days ago!" he assured us with glee.

"Are you sure it's the robbery money?" I asked, still uncertain if it was time to celebrate.

"I can read, can't I?" he countered. "Its got da right serial numbers on da bills, so it has ta be da money!"

"How do you know you got all of it?" I persisted in questioning. "You couldn't count it all?"

"Don't insult da Dink!" he shot back assuring us. "Havin' been in da money business, I knows what I'm talkin' 'bout, an' I saw enough of it ta know dats all of it! Plus da police has already counted it."

"How's that for a gully washer of joy!" Jasper added, getting in on the celebration now. "That's better news than a lightnin' bolt splittin' a frog pound!" he said, as he all of a sudden was spewing his Southern sayings again.

"I've got some more questions, Dink!" I said seriously, not wanting to curb the celebration, but wanting to be sure the celebration was based on truth.

"How does this help us put Sarah Sankster's sister away, and get Jasper released? Could it be that the minute she finds out the money is gone that she's gone too--- disappears never to be seen again, leaving Jasper to bear the blame for all these crimes that he's accused of now?"

But I wasn't finished yet.

"And by the way, Dink. Where and how did you get the money?" I asked, wondering if he was toying with me again in his slow release of the story.

"I got it from an old friend of years back---let's say, he's a money launderer---hot money, dat is? I tought dey might go ta him, or someone like him. So I put da word out to be on da watch fer it. Dat's where I been all day. I had ta drive ta Atlanta ta get it. I just now got back, an' came straight ta da jail. Sarah, Jr. and her boy friend took it by dis friend's place to exchange it fer cold money at da rate of three dollars to one. It seems dey was plannin' ta split."

"Okay, Dink. Let me see if I can line this up correctly. The police have the money. You can't implicate your money launderer in Atlanta, I would suppose," I said with some unbelief. "And now Sarah and her boyfriend have all the money they need, even at the reduced rate, and I'm sure they're on a plane right now to some distant place, free as a bird, and happy as lambs. Where does that leave us, and especially Jasper? What did the police say when you gave them the money?" I asked, feeling like I was pouring cold water on his plan and story.

It seemed to me we were getting in deeper and deeper with no way to extricate ourselves, especially Jasper. I really thought Dink had botched it this time!

"Oh, they're not goin' anywhere soon, 'cause they're in jail and have already confessed to the crimes!" he said, finally offering the punch line. "Jasper should be outta jail tomorrow!"

Well, those statements set off another celebration between Jasper and Dink! I concluded the others visiting the jail must have thought we had lost our minds! However, I still had some questions, and as I was stuck in Dink's game, I had to play it, and I knew he was enjoying every minute of it.

"Dink, I have some more questions. I will celebrate as much as anyone, once I know all the facts. So please, can we hold it down till we have the full story!" I pled, knowing I was at his mercy. I had to admit, if it was true, he had pulled off another one of his "miracles" when we seemed to be at a dead end. For that I was grateful for Jasper and Shirley's sake.

"Okay, Preacha, I'se been playin' witcha, I admit! But believe me, its all legit, and Jasper will be outta here by tomorrow! Guaranteed! And I will tell ya da rest of da story now!"

He preceded to unfold the reason Sarah's twin and her friend were now in jail, and singing like opera stars. It seemed that Sarah and her two friends had originally brought the twin sister and her friends into the deal, not to participate in the robbery, but to create confusion if suspicion ever came to Sarah. She would have an alibi for sure with her twin in another place. The twin and her friends were to get a million dollars between them, just to set up the alibi, and Sarah and her friends would have four million. But it seems greed set in, and the twin and her friends could not be satisfied with one million when they could have five million.

So the twin and her buddies killed Sarah and the two men, and blamed it on Jasper. They figured they were home free, except Sarah and her friends had hidden the money, and they couldn't find it. When we staked out the house, and called and told them someone knew where the money was, it spooked Bugsy, one of the twin's friends, and he took off. He wasn't going for the money, but for the airport, to get out of town, and away from what he felt would eventually come---blame for the various crimes. When we followed him, he panicked and crashed his car, accidentally killing himself.

The twin and her remaining friend finally found the remaining money. But fearing they might get caught and be prosecuted for the murder of Sarah and her friends, and maybe even for the murder of the armored car guard, a crime they hadn't committed, they sought to throw the authorities off by turning in a third of the money. They then took the other two thirds to Dink's money laundering friend, agreeing to less value for the "hot money," so they could leave town and have clean money to spend. But they never even got the clean money, as Dink's friend didn't want to be involved---the money was too hot, and he saw a chance to help Dink, returning previous favors, though Dink never told me what they were. The money launderer told them it would take him a day to get the clean money. But he insisted they leave the hot money with him, so he could count and inspect it.

The only thing is the twin and her friend didn't know that there was some incriminating evidence in one of the bags they brought to the hot money man. The third man of Sarah's group wrote a note before he was killed, in which he detailed the whole scheme, just in case the twin and her buddies pulled something, like getting rid of him, like they had killed Sarah and the other man, so they could have all the money. The note detailed the crimes, who had committed them, how Jasper had been framed, and even told where to find further evidence to corroborate the story. He knew it wouldn't matter if it was known they had committed the robbery and even killed the armored car guard, if the twin had pulled a fast one and gotten rid of them. You can't prosecute dead people, but dead people can get revenge on their betrayers. The motive for the letter was so that the twin and her buddies couldn't pull anything and get away with it.

When the money launderer saw the note, he showed it to Dink, and Dink called the police in the city where Jasper and Sarah had lived. He told them of the money and the new evidence. The police caught up with the twin and her boyfriend before they could get away, and they were now in jail in that town, awaiting further legal action. When told of the new evidence, each one of them began to talk, blaming the other one, trying to save his own skin.

When Dink was finished, we all let loose celebrating! Jasper called Shirley, and they cried together on the phone. It was almost too good to be true, in light of the fact it had come so fast. One minute it looked hopeless, and the next minute it was all over! But that's the way of the Lord!!!.

I talked to Ira, Jr., too. I'm not sure he understood the complicated events that had taken place. I'm not sure I did, exactly. He did remind me of our next goal.

"Daddy, now we can concentrate even more on praying for April! I really think she was better today!"

I wasn't sure if that was a fact or youthful hope buoyed by the events of the day. As I left the jail that night, I had one question---where are we going to meet for the rest of our study on salvation---my house or Jasper's house?

I liked those easy questions, after what we had been through!

36

What about I Corinthians 9:27?

It was late this Wednesday evening before we all got to bed, following a time of further celebration at the hospital. And sure enough, Jasper was freed the next day, a Thursday, as Dink had promised. He was at the hospital when we arrived. Shirley was with him, and it was clear that their relationship was on the way to full restoration, probably to be stronger than ever before. They had hopes that Shirley could go home very soon, though they would still put in much of their time at the hospital, until April came out of the coma.

Part of our agreement had been that we would take a break each evening while young Ira and I visited April, and we would continue our doctrinal discussion of salvation. So about 7:00 PM we headed for the cafeteria area to eat a bite and continue our pursuit.

"I want us to look today at one of the most difficult of all the passages of the Bible---a key passage in our discussion of whether one can lose his salvation or not. The passage is I Corinthians 9:27."

I read the passage for us as follows:

But I keep under my body, and bring it into subjection, lest that by any means, when I have preached to others, I myself should be a castaway.

I pointed out to Jasper that some interpret this verse to mean that one could lose his salvation. Thus, according to this view, Paul is saying that he disciplines his body because he is fearful that having been active in ministry, he might in the end be rejected of God, having lost his salvation, because of a lack of discipline and an indulgent attitude towards sin. The word used by Paul here is adokimos, and it carries the following meanings:

to not stand the test
to fail to be approved
to become disapproved
to become unfit
to become spurious
to become reprobate
to become a castaway
to become rejected
to become unapproved
to become worthless

Thus the conclusion cannot be made immediately that this verse speaks of the loss of one's salvation. There are some guiding factors which we must remember before jumping to any such conclusion. Notice two of those guiding hermeneutical factors:

1. Like Hebrews 6:4-6, this is a very difficult passage. Thus, the hermeneutical (interpretative) principle that we must follow is that we must build a doctrine on the easier passages (those we have already shown which teach one cannot lose salvation) rather than to build a doctrine on the more difficult and obscure passages (such as the Hebrews passage or even this passage).

2. The context of any passage is central and supreme in interpreting it, and therefore, we must carefully consider the context of I Corinthians 9:27 before we even begin to try to understand its meaning.

Thus I noted with Jasper the following context of the difficult verse before us.

THE OVERALL TEXT IN CONTEXT FOR THE INTERPRETAION OF I CORINTHIANS 9:27

I THE CORINTHIANS WERE IMMATURE IN THEIR FELLOWSHIP (Chapters 1-4)

They had divisions because they were focused upon men rather than upon Christ

II THE CORINTHIANS WERE IMMATURE IN THEIR VIEWS OF MORALITY (Chapter 5)

They allowed immorality to exist in their membership when they should have practiced church discipline.

III THE CORINTHIANS WERE IMMATURE IN THEIR UNDERSTANDING OF RELATING TO ONE ANOTHER BEFORE THE WORLD (Chapter 6)

They were taking one another to court

IV THE CORINTHIANS WERE IMMATURE IN THEIR VIEW OF LIBERTY (Chapter 6)

They were feeling a tension between freedom and responsibility

V THE CORINTHIANS WERE IMMATURE IN THEIR VIEWS OF MARRIAGE   (Chapter 7)

They were wrestling with several questions about marriage:

> celibacy versus marrying
> separation and remarriage
> remaining with a lost mate
> deciding to marry in a time of distress
> children's marriages

VI THE CORINTHIANS WERE IMMATURE IN THEIR UNDERSTANDING OF TRUE CHRISTIAN LIBERTY   Chapters. 8-10

Chapter 8---the eating of meat offered to idols
Chapter 9---the example of the Apostle Paul

A. The freedom of Paul---the ground   9:1-2

> he is an apostle   1
> he is free   1
> he is an eyewitness of Christ   1
> he has spiritual fruit---the Corinthians   1-2
> > they are the seal of his apostleship in the Lord

B. The freedom of Paul---the areas   9:3-14

> he is free to eat (that which is offered to idols)   4

he is free to drink (that which is offered to idols) 4
he is free to marry and take a wife with him 5
he is free to forbear working 6-14

C. The freedom of Paul forfeited 9:15-23

he does not claim any of these freedoms 15
he does not write now to claim them 15
he would rather die than claim them 15
he does not preach for financial gain 16-17
he preaches for a different gain 18
he serves forfeiting his rights and freedom 19-23

D. The freedom of Paul---exhortations 9:24-27

Paul is not commanding others
    to forfeit their freedom in all areas
Paul is forfeiting his in light of the Christian race

1. There is a race to be run---a prize to be won 24
2. There is a discipline required 25-27

Paul runs in a spiritual race 26
Paul runs with a goal 24-25
    that he may obtain 24
        an incorruptible crown
    not as one who beats the air 26
Paul runs with discipline 27
    he keeps his body in subjection
    he is fearful of falling out of the race
        this is not the loss of salvation
        this is failure in ministry

Summary

Paul has forfeited his freedom, yea, his legitimate Christian freedom in some areas, not that he might be saved, but that he might run the Christian race in a better manner. His fear is not that he would lose his salvation, but that he might not run the Christian race to the fullest for the glory of God, and thus forfeit the incorruptible crown.

Paul does not lay these convictions by way of commandments upon others. All believers are free to practice proper Christian freedom. But in the process they must also run the Christian race to the fullest. The context of Christian liberty will not allow us to apply this verse to salvation. If the matter in sight here were salvation, Paul would have commanded all to follow his example.

The admonition is for believers to be careful of abusing their Christian freedom, even at times a legitimate freedom, in light of weightier matters, such as the weak brother in Christ, and the seriousness of the race we are running for eternity.

Thus the loss Paul fears here is not salvation, but the faithfulness which is required for the greatest glory to God and eternal reward for service.

With our study and light supper over, we went back up to April's room. We hadn't expected our joy to be so rudely and sadly interrupted as it was when we entered her room.

37

Why All This Waiting?

The euphoria of the previous hours was soon turned into deep sorrow, when we returned to April's hospital room. She had to be taken to emergency surgery, because of a complication in her brain area. She had experienced a seizure, and upon examination, it was determined the surgery was absolutely necessary for survival. Even with the surgery, there was an uncertainty that she would live.

We found everyone in prayer in the chapel of the operating area of the hospital. So we knelt and joined them, and we remained for an extended period of time, pouring out our hearts for a dearly beloved little girl.

When our prayer time was ended, I was particularly concerned about Jasper, Shirley, and young Ira. Jasper was encouraging Shirley, so I turned to Ira to see how he was doing.

"Are you alright?" I asked.

"There's not much to encourage us, is there, Daddy? Except our trust in the Lord! I guess sometimes the Lord wants to see if we are really trusting in Him or in the circumstances around us."

"That's right, son!" I agreed. "God wants us to trust Him regardless---regardless of the circumstances, the pain, the uncertainty, the tears or the sorrow. He wants us to trust Him to do what is best, and He is the only one who knows what is best for us in every circumstance. We may think we know what is best, but He wants us to trust Him to bring to pass what he knows is best, even if we do not want it and do not understand it, when it does come to pass."

"That's real faith, isn't it Daddy?" he offered.

"Yes, that's the ultimate in faith---something we all struggle to reach, in light of our weaknesses in the flesh!" I explained.

"I've sure got that, Daddy---what you call a weakness in the flesh!"

The operation took a number of hours, and when they had finished, the doctor said we would just have to wait and see. He could give no assurance one way or the other. I knew I needed to get young Ira home, but he wanted to remain, and Jasper and Shirley wanted us both to stay, so we agreed, hoping to see some progress during the night.

It was a time when everyone just sat silently waiting. You didn't feel like eating, or studying, or thinking---only praying in our own hearts, and from time to time praying together again. As we waited, I recorded some thoughts for my own edification.

We are a hasty people.

We are always in a hurry.

We cannot wait for anything---food, traffic, lines at
    places of business, other people, etc.

We are a do-it-now generation, an I-must-have-
    everything-now people, I-cannot-wait-for-anything
    kind of society.

God can wait on us, but God forbid that He would ever
    require that we wait on Him for anything.

Much of our trouble in life comes from our impatience,
    our hastiness, our let's-get-on-with-it attitude.

This is particularly difficult when it comes to prayer. Surely God could tell us immediately how all our problems and troubles are going to work out, if He wanted to do so. So let's blame God for His delays. We haven't got the time or the stomach for it.

But in reality, God often walks slower than we do! We insist on running ahead of Him in our self-will and know-it-all attitude. He realizes the discipline of time. We hate the discipline of time. He wills and works the best---in His time. We want to do something in every situation---anything, just so something is accomplished. And when we do act in this hurried setting, we then insist He put His stamp of approval on it, even if it was the wrong thing.

In reality, He is often waiting on us to ask Him, to seek Him, to surrender to Him. But we are so busy with our thinking about what we must do, or what He should do, that we don't have time to ask, seek or surrender.

And when we go forward without Him, do we not leave the blessing behind too, as we keep telling God to hurry up and catch up with us?

Thus there are times to go forward and there are times to wait upon Him. But it seems the only time we will wait is when we must. In most other situations we must do something, even if it is the wrong thing.

May God give us the wisdom to know when to act, and when to wait, especially in those other times, when doing something is possible but uncertain to us.

When young Ira read the above thoughts, he exclaimed, "Daddy, someday you need to write a book about this experience in our lives!"

38

Is It Really Continuation Salvation?

When no word came by 1:00 AM, I realized it would be difficult, but I had to take young Ira home. He was reluctant to go, but knew in his heart that it was a necessity, as April might linger in this condition for a long time. I instructed him on the way home that he was to sleep late the next morning, and we would go to the hospital about 11:00 AM the next day. I would get a sub for my classes.

I got up the next morning about 7:00 AM, long enough to call a fellow professor named Purvis McSwain, and he agreed to cover my classes for me. He was about my age, a good scholar, and a very helpful friend to me during this first semester of my teaching. He, along with my pastor, Bo Hayden, had made the adjustment from pastoral life to academic life much easier than I had expected.

When I got up about mid-morning, I called the hospital, and Shirley informed me that there was no change in April's condition. She had sent Jasper home about 3:00 AM, while she stayed. She expected him back about noon, and she was going home for some rest then, since the doctor had released her, not only because of the improvement of her condition, but also because of the circumstances.

We arrived at the hospital a little before noon, and Jasper was there also. We prayed together again, and since no one else was in the chapel, we decided to enjoin our doctrinal pursuit once again. Young Ira remained with us, knowing that visits to intensive care would be periodic, and that we could break at the appointed time to cover them. Any other change would be relayed to us in the chapel.

I noted for Jasper that some of the verses used by those believing one can lose salvation are actually teaching perseverance and not teaching one can be lost after being saved. I noted an example of these verses for him.

John 8:51

> *Verily, verily, I say unto you, If a man keep my saying, he shall never see death.*

In light of what the Bible says clearly about salvation, as we have seen previously, this verse must be teaching perseverance. Keeping Christ's saying is the proof of salvation. To read it any other way, that is to make the keeping of Christ's saying the basis of never seeing death, would be to base never seeing death on the ground of the work of keeping His saying.

I noted further some other verses that were used to state one could lose their salvation

Luke 8:13---The Lord's Parable of the Sower

> *13 They on the rock are they who, when they hear, receive the word with joy; and these have no root, who for a while believe, and in time of temptation fall away. 15 But that on the good ground are they who, in an honest and good heart, having heard the word, keep it, and bring forth fruit with patience.*

verse 13
>these people (they on the rock) did the following:
>>they heard the word
>>they received the word with joy
>>they had no root and believed for awhile
>>they fell away in a time of temptation
>the explanation needed to understand this passage
>>the hearing of the word obviously does not save
>>the receiving of the word with joy says too little
>>the believing for awhile does not equal salvation
>>>see John 2:23 where it says many believed
>>>>in His name when they saw the miracles
>>>>which He did
>>>>but Jesus didn't commit himself to them
>>>>because He knew all men
>>>>because He knew what was in men
>>>thus here in John 2:23 is a believing
>>>>that is not a saving faith
>>the real key to the passage is "they had no root"
>thus there is a false faith
>>which receives the word
>>>in a shallow rootless manner
>>which may appear to men to be true faith
>>which in time will be shown to be a false faith
>>>because it had no root
>>>because it was an external reception
>>>because it never took root in the inner man

verse 15
>those on the good ground
>>are they who in an honest and good heart
>>>who having heard the word keep it
>>>who bring forth fruit with patience
>>are the truly saved as they persevere

Thus these verses do not teach one can lose salvation
but that the truly saved will persevere in faith.

Luke 11:28

*But He said, Yes, rather, blessed are they that hear the
word of God, and keep it.*

Those who believe one can lose his salvation think this
verse teaches that the individual who faithfully keeps
the word of God after being saved, is the one who
continues to be saved. In reality all the verse says is
that the one who hears the word and keeps it is blessed
(the word blessed does not mean to be saved).

Luke 12:46---The Lord's Parable of Servanthood

*The Lord of that servant will come in a day when he
looks not for him, and at an hour when he is not aware,
and will cut him in sunder, and will appoint him his
portion with the unbelievers.*

This parable tells the story of a servant (some think it
speaks of two servants). It simply states that the
servant has two choices in serving his master in his
absence: to be faithful or to be unfaithful. If the
servant is faithful, he will be rewarded positively. If he
is unfaithful, he will be rewarded negatively, by being
cut in sunder, and by being given his part with the
unbelievers.

The one who believes this teaches loss of salvation
argues that the servant is a saved man who has his

choice of continuing to be saved and finding reward, or of not continuing in salvation and facing judgment with other unbelievers (the adikios). Thus continuing in salvation is based on faithfulness in servanthood.

First, let it be noted that it is wiser to use the didactic passages to build doctrine, rather than try to build doctrine in detail from a parable, since parables are more difficult to interpret, and since they normally stress one clear basic truth.

Second, the teaching of the passage that is consistent with the rest of Scripture that we have been considering, as well as with the context of this passage, is that the faithful steward, because he gives evidence that he is truly a believer, will be rewarded, and the unfaithful steward, as he gives evidence he is not a true believer will receive his part with the unbelievers, because that is what he is. It merely confirms the doctrine of the perseverance of the true believer once again, while the lack of perseverance of the one who professes falsely.

Realizing our time was slipping away, I made some final conclusions.

1. There is no end to difficult passages which one will face concerning this subject. One could entangle himself endlessly trying to answer them all.

2. The better approach is to do what we have already done, that is, to understand what salvation really is through the study of the doctrine of salvation as a

whole---regeneration, justification by faith, etc. That is, study the whole of Scripture, and establish that salvation is by grace through faith alone and not by works. Then approach the difficult passages.

3. There are passages of warning to the believer throughout Scripture to persevere. Do not turn these passages into warnings that one can lose his salvation. The believer does need to hear of the necessity of perseverance as the evidence and proof of a true faith.

4. There is a dangerous and subtle error made when one takes verses of Scripture that are warnings to persevere and turns them into statements that one can lose his salvation. That error is that continuation in the Christian life (works) becomes the basis of salvation, rather than the continuation in the Christian life being the evidence of true salvation. If one is saved as long as he continues in the Christian life, that is salvation by works. If continuation in the Christian life is the evidence of salvation, that is salvation by grace, then it is grace that saves and keeps one in the pathway of righteousness.

5. Remember that not all who profess to be saved are really saved, thus we see the necessity of the warnings to persevere. Therefore, it is not that all who profess are truly saved, and then the ones who turn back are lost again. It is that some who profess are really saved, and they will evidence that true profession by perseverance, while the others who profess have not truly been saved at all, and they are the ones who turn back.

6. Remember that distinguishing the two (that is, the true profession from the false profession) is not always easy, nor can it be done in a day or a year, for even true Christians can fail, and sometimes miserably. It may take several years to see if one possesses true salvation. But a good rule is to note that the longer a professing Christian continues to live in rebellion against God without chastisement from God, then the bigger the question mark becomes beside his profession of faith.

Jasper thanked me once again, not only for these studies, but for standing with him through his time of stumbling before the Lord.

I could tell also that Ira had enjoyed the theological pursuit, as his young voice began to lead us in Amazing Grace! There were only three of us, but our voices filled the chapel as we praised Him for a salvation that is by grace and not dependent upon our puny and worthless works, for if that were the case we would never make it. We could no more in our own strength keep ourselves saved, than we could save ourselves to begin with. How comforting to know that in a changing world, there is one thing that will stand for eternity---our standing before God by faith alone in Jesus Christ! We are secure because of the work and righteousness of Jesus Christ---not because of our works.

Not only did music fill the room and our hearts, but tears filled our eyes, as we sang:

Amazing grace, how sweet the sound,
That saved a wretch like me.
I once was lost, but now am found,
Was blind but now I see.

39

What Is Glorification?

After our study and time of praise and prayer, we went back to the waiting room for intensive care patients. Shirley was there by now, and we could do nothing but wait, and doze off and on, since the night had been so short. The only one who seemed to have much energy that day was Ira, Jr.

Thus it is no surprise that around 1:30 PM he poked me from my half-awake or half-asleep slumber (call it what you will), and pointed down the hall.

"Daddy, there's the doctor! He's coming towards us! Maybe he has some word on April!"

We all jumped to our feet, as Jasper and Shirley had been stirred as well, and walked towards him.

"I have some good news!" he said. "She's well enough to go back to a private room, but we still don't know anything about the length of the coma. That is out of our hands!"

This was good news, for which we were grateful, as it meant that she was improving and out of immediate danger. It also meant that we could be with her all the time, as before, to speak to her and encourage her, but we had no idea when the coma might end! But again, what else might develop to threaten her existence? So we waited, dependant on the Lord!

Young Ira continued his incessant talking to her, not caring that she could not answer. It made him feel better, and as he said, "Who knows whether it just might help her in some way."

About 5:00 PM Jasper and I went down to the hospital cafeteria for supper and to discuss another of our doctrinal subjects---the glorification of the believer. We needed all the encouragement and spiritual enlightenment we could get!

The passage we were going to consider on glorification was Romans 8:29-30, which reads as follows:

29 For whom he did foreknow, he also did predestinate to be conformed to the image of His Son, that He might be the firstborn among many brethren. 30 Moreover, whom He did predestinate, them he also called; and whom he called, them he also justified; and whom he justified, them he also glorified.

I told Jasper that this is what I call the golden link of guaranteed salvation to God's elect:

I   THE TEXT SAYS

whom God did foreknow
   He predestinated
      to be conformed to the image of His son
whom God predestinated
   them He also called
whom God called
   them He also justified
whom God justified
   them He also glorified

II THE TEXT TEACHES

God <u>foreknew</u> individuals!
    (the word whom here is singular)
God <u>predestinated</u> individuals
    based on His foreknowledge
    to be conformed to the image of Christ
    that he might be the firstborn
        among many brethren!
    (the word whom here is singular also)
    (the word them is plural)
God <u>called</u> individuals!
    based on the predestination
    (the word whom here is singular again)
    (the word them is plural)
God <u>justified</u> individuals!
    based on the calling
    (the word whom here is singular as well)
    (the word them is plural)
God glorified individuals!
    based on the justification
    (the word whom here is singular also)
    (the word them is plural)

III THE TEXT SUMMARIZED

Thus it is clear that God has a people
    but individuals are part of that group
    based on God's work of salvation
    procured for each individual of the group
        through this golden link of salvation
            foreknowing
            predestination

        calling
        justification
        glorification

IV THE TERMS OF THE TEXT DEFINED

A. Foreknowledge

This is not merely prescience
    that is to know something before hand
This speaks of entering into a relationship
    with the people known as His elect
For a full discussion of this passage
    see *A Journey in Grace*, pp. 56-58

B. Predestination

This is the predestination of those foreknown
    to be become like Christ
        through the work of salvation

C. Calling

This is the effectual calling
    of those foreknown and predestinated
Since they are foreknown and predestinated
    they will be called

D. Justification

This is the declaring of the called (the elect)
    as righteous before God
    based on the work of Christ for them

E. Glorification---see the following discussion

V GLORIFICATION

A. <u>Glorification is but the climax of the work of God for us</u>

> 1. *God completes His work of salvation for the elect by glorification*

> 2. *God's completion of His work of salvation by glorification is certain*

> as we see in the golden link of salvation
> > each work is a work of God
> > and is not left to the will or work of man

> 3   *God's completion of His work in glorification climaxes all His previous work*

> <u>foreknowing</u> us began the work of salvation
> > we could not foreknow ourselves
> <u>predestination</u> guarantees His work in us
> > we could not predestinate ourselves
> <u>effectual calling</u> brings us to Him
> > we could not call ourselves
> > we could not break the power of sin
> <u>justification</u> allows Him to accept us
> > as He declares us righteous
> > > on the basis of the righteousness
> > > > of Christ by faith alone
> > we could not justify ourselves

glorification brings us to heaven
     in the fullness of the image of Christ
         something which we could not do
         something which awaits His time
             the Second Coming of Christ
             the resurrection of the saints
   when the perfection of body and being
     in every way and every part
     is ours for eternity
  when we are done with sin in every way
    so that we can mirror in fullness
         the glorious image of Christ
    so that we can worship in fullness
         the great God of our salvation
  when we are in every way and every part
    exactly what God wants us to be
         in nature
         in action
         in thought, deed, and word

B. <u>The text puts it in the past tense though it is a future event because of the certainty of it fulfillment</u>

   it is the predestined work of God to come
   it is called by some theologians
     an eternal glorification
     due to its certainty
     based on salvation by grace

As we came to a close, I thought Jasper would explode with praise!

"I never saw all that before, Ira! Wow! I'm changing my old Arminian mantra from 'Saved, sanctified, livin' above sin, and striven to go in' to 'Saved, justified, and waitin' to be glorified!'"

"And add, 'And all by grace alone!'" I suggested.

About this time, the hospital paged us, and asked us to return to April's room. We both concluded something big must be up! But what? Good news or bad news?

As we stepped into the elevator, I quoted a poem I had learned some years back, trusting God would use it to comfort our hearts:

I know not, but God knows:
O blessed rest from fear!
All our unfolding days,
To Him are plain and clear.
Each anxious, puzzled "Why?"
From doubt or dread that grows,
Finds answer in this thought:
I know not, but He knows!
(Author Unknown)

40

What Can We Do But Praise Him?

Shirley was standing outside the door waiting for us, when we arrived. She was quite excited!

"April stirred just a few minutes ago, as if she might come out of the coma! Ira's in there talking to her now---even more than he did before!" she explained.

We went in, and sure enough there he was, talking up a storm. I never expected such a quiet boy could have so much to say, especially at such a moment as this. He was standing on a chair, leaning over the bed, giving everything he had in his speech of assurance and reminiscence. I thought, just like a good Calvinist---trust God to do His work, but don't neglect our responsibility.

Jasper and Shirley moved in close to monitor her every breath and potential move. They were content to let young Ira have the floor in this crucial moment.

Then it happened! April opened her eyes, looked around a few seconds, and then spoke in her southern drawl.

"Ira Pointer, seems like I've been hearing you talk for days now!" she said with a smile. "I never knew you were that much of an orator! Not that I don't like what you said ---telling me I'm the prettiest girl you know! And asking me not to leave you? Where in the world did you think I was going? And saying all those things in front of my daddy and mommy, kind of embarrassed me a little!"

Then it hit her!

"Daddy, what are you doing here? I thought you were in jail! Jesus did answer our prayers for you, didn't He! And you've got your arm around mommy and you're huggin' her! Jesus really answered our prayers!" she continued, as she looked back at Ira, as tears came to her eyes.

Tears filled all of our eyes! Young Ira, being the spokesman, sought to explain everything to her as briefly as possible. She listened intently, and seemed to understand some things, but still grimaced in thought to grasp the whole experience.

Then she spoke again.

"Ira, do you love Jesus? I love Jesus! Do you?"

To which Ira replied, "Yes, April, I love Jesus too! And I think we need to thank Him for all He has done! For you, April! For your mommy and daddy! And for saving us with a salvation by grace alone---a salvation which we will never lose! He will keep us forever!!!"

And what a time of rejoicing and prayer was ours! It will have to be a super time in heaven to beat this moment!!

In the days that followed, April recovered fully from her injuries. Jasper and Shirley re-established their home on a solid Christian foundation. Eventually, Jasper, after several years of restoration, took another pastorate---in Georgia. And young Ira kept up his friendship with April, which necessitated frequent trips for all of us to Georgia (until he was old enough to drive himself). And the child's love they had for one another? It also in time grew into courtship and even a deeper love, which then understandably led to wedding bells!

But all of that's another story!

ENDNOTES

Chapter 1

[1]In the last book of this series, *A Journey in Eschatology* (Richbarry Press, 2000), the main character, Pastor Ira Pointer, was invited in the Spring of 1982 to join the faculty of Evangelistic Baptist Seminary. He waited till the Spring of 1983 to accept this invitation and join the faculty in the Fall of 1983.

Chapter 2

[1]In another book of this series, *A Journey in Providence* (Richbarry Press, 1999), Dink and his wife Janie, lost their son by a kidnapping.

Chapter 11

[1]The same issue and reference as in footnote one in Chapter 2.

Chapter 21

[1]The same issue and reference as in footnotes in Chapters 2 and 11.

Chapter 22

[1]There are several ways in Judo to choke an opponent. One is to compress the carotid arteries on one or both sides of the neck. This restricts the flow of blood and oxygen to the brain. This is easier, safer and brings less pain than other methods and leaves the opponent unconscious for a short period of time.

Chapter 23

[1]Kittel, Gerhard, Editor, *Theological Dictionary of the New Testament, Vol. IV* (Grand Rapids: Eerdmans Publishing Company), pp. 976-980.
[2]Ibid., pp. 980-988.
[3]Ibid., pp. 999-1103
[4]Vine, W.E., *An Expository Dictionary of New Testament Words* (Fleming H. Revell Company), p. 281.
[5]Arndt, William F. and F. Wilbur Gingrich, *A Greek-English Lexicon of the New Testament and Other Early Christian Literature* (Chicago: University of Chicago Press, 1952), pp. 512-514.

Chapter 24

[1]Richard P. Belcher, *A Journey in Inspiration* (Columbia, SC: Richbarry Press, 1998), pp. 140-146.